Dearest Father,

Think of me when you read this book and remember me with a smile of happiness, knowing that I am waiting for you — forever.

Yours, forever,

Punky

TO ABSENT FRIENDS

A Collection of Stories of the Dogs We Miss

TO ABSENT FRIENDS

A Collection of Stories of the Dogs We Miss

COMPILED BY JAMESON PARKER

Willow Creek
PRESS

Published by Willow Creek Press
P.O. Box 147, Minocqua, Wisconsin 54548
www.willowcreekpress.com

ISBN 1-57223-706-6

Printed in Canada

For Judith, with love and gratitude.

TABLE OF CONTENTS

INTRODUCTION

THERE HAVE BEEN DOGS in my life since long before I was in it. My father loved dogs, and the dogs of his childhood and young manhood are as real to me as if the memories of them were my own, ghosts of ghosts that I can call by name and summon to my side.

I have a photograph of my father at eight or nine holding Brownie, the non-descript spaniel who was party to the breaking of a valuable vase my father took the punishment for. And it was Brownie who was the unwilling recipient of an entire bottle of expensive imported perfume after my grandmother complained of the little dog's smell.

I see Lady Rose, the white collie, hurling herself with reckless courage at a pair of Chows that attacked my teenaged father. And I see, too, Lady Rose being smuggled into that dark old Maryland house to sleep on my father's bed.

There is Ding, the eponymous Chesapeake Bay retriever that Ding Darling gave to my father as a wedding present.

Ding never could learn, despite all evidence to the contrary, that my father really was an excellent swimmer and didn't need to be saved. Ding, who did learn to retrieve the morning paper and then had to be painstakingly taught not to retrieve *every* paper in Dickyville. I see Ding as an old dog, with a prime roast of beef (this was during the war when meat was rationed) held firmly in his jaws, running down the streets of Dickyville pursued by my Aunt's unloved and unwanted suitor, butcher knife in his hand, as Aunt Kitty and my father clung to each other, helpless with laughter.

These gentle ghosts push their way in to be petted in their turn beside other, more recent friends.

After I was born, on one of his overseas tours of duty, my father somehow acquired a Boxer from the police department in the then small German village of Bad Godesberg. The police were getting rid of the dog because they couldn't break him of brawling, and by the time my father got him, one eye had been ripped out in a fight and the skin sewn shut over the vacant cavity, giving him a decidedly piratical look. One ear had been torn and hung down at a jaunty angle. His massive head was a memory album of his many encounters, a roadmap of cicatrices. All this and he was not yet three.

But Egon was a fully-trained police dog and he took his new duties — protecting my sister and me from the trashy riffraff of lawyers and lobbyists who lived on our street in Washington, D.C. — very seriously.

When Egon and I were both about eight or nine we were allowed to extend the range of our travels to the wilds of

Rock Creek Park. Sometimes I fished in that creek, catching nothing; mostly I just played and explored.

It was on one of these jaunts, while Egon was busy off in the bushes keeping the world safe from squirrels, that I was approached by a man. He was very nice. He knew how to speak to little boys easily and familiarly, how to take an interest in their activities, the games they might be playing, to point out things they would almost certainly be interested in.

And yet, and yet... I remember how, as he bent over, hands on his knees, to bring his face closer to mine, I knew, with a cymbal clash of recognition, what he was and what he wanted. I had no previous knowledge or conception of it — such things were not common enough to merit discussion in nice, safe, middle-class houses in the fifties — let alone words for it, but I knew absolutely and positively. So I was ready, and when he grabbed me I screamed.

The sight of the thing that came out of the bushes when I screamed, one gleaming eye filled with rage and mayhem, huge jaws open and roaring, ears pinned back against the scarred head, eighty-five pounds of superbly-trained aggression, must have seemed apocalyptic to that man. In my memory he simply rose, softly and gracefully, into the upper reaches of a nearby tree, settling birdlike on a branch. I know his actual ascent must have been more painful, and costly to his suit, but that's not how I remember it. Egon raged beneath the tree, tearing at the bark with those awesome teeth. If I hadn't leashed him and dragged him off he would have chewed that tree down eventually.

Egon saved me two other times. He saved my father's life

once. But how I remember him most clearly is on his back on my bed, all four legs in the air, snoring loudly and happily.

Roger was a bullmastiff who my mother, absentminded under the best of circumstances, consistently confused with me. I was scolded for doing things on the living room rug that were better done outside. Roger was implored to help her find her glasses. I have enriched the lives of several psychiatrists trying to explain this.

North, a dignified and gentle collie, and Tasha, a blind Briard, helped me through college. And North helped me later through some very bad and difficult times following the sudden, violent death of my father. North's magnificent white ruff absorbed a lot of tears.

Max, a Chesapeake Bay retriever, ambassador for the breed, taught me with love, and patience better than my own, as much about the training of dogs as any book I ever read, any expert I ever questioned. He taught me, too, far more about hunting than I ever taught him.

Daisy, a gallant, crippled Gordon setter who hunted her heart out for the love of the game and for the love of me. Scout, Cody, Biscuit...

They all gather by my pillow at night, these beloved ghosts. If I loved them all, it was nothing to the love they gave me.

But I am not an indiscriminate lover of dogs. A dog is like a spouse: that special person who makes your life worth living might make me run screaming into the night. Just so with dogs. The wildly eccentric hunting dog who shares my life just now, a Pudelpointer named Liberty, might make you take up serious competitive drinking, but he suits me just fine. It is not the dog, it's *your* dog, and the common experiences and emotions that come from a life shared with dogs. Those experiences, those emotions, transcend all the petty, mundane, and artificial barriers that the vain and insecure human animal erects in his effort to build himself up: race, religion, nationality, wealth, social status, profession, political affiliation, sex. None of these amounts to a hill of beans to a dog. He gives all of himself — his love, his too-short life — unconditionally, without judgment or censure. A homeless person's dog will defend his owner against Bill Gates or the Prince of Wales or the President of the United States just as vigorously as Egon defended me all those years ago.

We seem incapable, sometimes, of learning from our dogs and following their good example, but we can honor their memories. The dogs in these pages might not have suited you, or me. But they suited someone, and now the memories of them are honored in the telling of their stories. Maybe their stories will remind you of an absent friend.

Jameson Parker
July, 2003

THE POWER OF THE DOG

Rudyard Kipling

There is sorrow enough in the natural way
From men and women to fill our day;
But when we are certain of sorrow in store,
Why do we always arrange for more?
Brothers and sisters, I bid you beware
Of giving your heart to a dog to tear.

Buy a puppy and your money will buy
Love unflinching that cannot lie —
Perfect passion and worship fed
By a kick in the ribs or a pat on the head.
Nevertheless it is hardly fair
To risk your heart for a dog to tear.

When the fourteen years which Nature permits
Are closing in asthma, or tumour, or fits,
And the vet's unspoken prescription runs
To lethal chambers or loaded guns,
Then you will find — it's your own affair,
But... you've given your heart to a dog to tear.

When the body that lived at your single will,
When the whimper of welcome is stilled (how still),
When the spirit that answered your every mood
Is gone — wherever it goes — for good,
You will discover how much you care,
And will give your heart to a dog to tear!

We've sorrow enough in the natural way,
When it comes to burying Christian clay.
Our loves are not given, but only lent,
At compound interest of cent per cent.
Though it is not always the case, I believe,
That the longer we've kept 'em, the more do we grieve.
For when debts are payable, right or wrong,
A short-time loan is as bad as a long.
So why in Heaven (before we are there!)
Should we give our hearts to a dog to tear?

A SNAPSHOT OF REX

James Thurber

I RAN ACROSS A dim photograph of him the other day, going through some old things. He's been dead about forty years. His name was Rex (my two brothers and I named him when we were in our early teens) and he was a bull terrier. "An American bull terrier," we used to say, proudly; none of your English bulls. He had one brindle eye that sometimes made him look like a clown and sometimes reminded you of a politician with derby hat and cigar. The rest of him was white except for a brindle saddle that always seemed to be slipping off and a brindle stocking on a hind leg. Neverthe-less, there was a nobility about him. He was big and muscular and beautifully made. He never lost his dignity even when trying to accomplish the extravagant tasks my brothers and I used to set for him. One of these was the bringing of a ten-foot wooden rail into the yard through the back gate. We would throw it out into the alley and tell him to go get it. Rex was as powerful as a wrestler, and there were not many things that he couldn't manage somehow to get hold of with his great jaws and lift or drag to wherever he wanted to put them, or wherever we wanted them put. He would catch the rail at the balance and lift it clear of the ground and trot with great confidence toward the gate. Of course, since the gate was only four feet wide or so, he couldn't bring the rail in broadside. He found that out when he got a few terrific jolts, but he wouldn't give up. He finally figured out how to do it, by dragging the rail, holding onto one end, growling. He got a great, wagging satisfaction out of his work. We used to bet kids who had never seen Rex in action that he could catch a baseball thrown as high as they could throw it. He almost never let us down. Rex could hold a baseball with ease in his mouth, in one cheek, as if it were a chew of tobacco.

He was a tremendous fighter, but he never started fights. I don't believe he liked to get into them, despite the fact that he came from a line of fighters. He never went for another dog's throat but for one of its ears (that teaches a dog a lesson), and he would get his grip, close his eyes, and hold on. He could hold on for hours. His longest fight lasted from dusk until almost pitch-dark, one Sunday. It was fought in East Main Street in Columbus with a large, snarly nondescript that belonged to a big colored man. When Rex finally got his ear grip, the brief whirlwind of snarling turned to screeching. It was frightening to listen to and to watch. The Negro boldly picked the dogs up somehow and began swinging them around his head, and finally let them fly like a hammer in a hammer throw, but although they landed ten feet away with a great plump, Rex still held on.

The two dogs eventually worked their way to the middle of the car tracks, and after a while two or three streetcars were held up by the fight. A motorman tried to pry Rex's jaws open with a switch rod; somebody lighted a fire and made a torch of a stick and held that to Rex's tail, but he paid no attention. In the end, all the residents and storekeepers in the neighborhood were on hand, shouting this, suggesting that. Rex's joy of battle, when battle was joined, was almost tranquil. He had a kind of pleasant expression during fights, not a vicious one, his eyes closed in what would have seemed to be sleep had it not been for the turmoil of the struggle. The Oak Street Fire Depart-ment finally had to be sent for — I don't know why nobody thought of it sooner. Five or six pieces of apparatus arrived, followed by a battalion chief. A hose was attached and a powerful stream of water was turned on the dogs. Rex held on for several moments more while the torrent buffeted him about like a log in a freshet. He was a hundred yards away from where the fight started when he finally let go.

The story of that Homeric fight got all around town, and some of our relatives looked upon the incident as a blot on the family name. They insisted that we get rid of Rex, but we were very happy with him, and nobody could have made us give him up. We would have left town with him first, along any road there was to go. It would have been different, perhaps, if he had ever started fights, or looked for trouble.

But he had a gentle disposition. He never bit a person in the ten strenuous years that he lived, nor ever growled at anyone except prowlers. He killed cats, that is true, but quickly and neatly and without especial malice, the way men kill certain animals. It was the only thing he did that we could never cure him of doing. He never killed or even chased a squirrel. I don't know why. He had his own philosophy about such things. He never ran barking after wagons or automobiles. He didn't seem to see the idea in pursuing something you couldn't catch, or something you couldn't do anything with, even if you did catch it. A wagon was one of the things he couldn't tug along with his mighty jaws, and he knew it. Wagons, therefore, were not a part of his world.

Swimming was his favorite recreation. The first time he ever saw a body of water (Alum Creek), he trotted nervously along the steep bank for a while, fell to barking wildly, and finally plunged in from a height of eight feet or more. I shall always remember that shining, virgin dive. Then he swam upstream and back just for the pleasure of it, like a man. It was fun to see him battle upstream against a stiff current, struggling and growling every foot of the way. He had as much fun in the water as any person I have known. You didn't have to throw a stick in the water to get him to go in. Of course, he would bring back a stick to you if you did throw one in. He would even have brought back a piano if you had thrown one in.

That reminds me of the night, way after midnight, when he went a-roving in the light of the moon and brought back a small chest of drawers that he had found somewhere — how far from the house nobody ever knew; since it was Rex, it could easily have been half a mile. There were no drawers in the chest when he got it home, and it wasn't a good one — he hadn't taken it out of anybody's house; it was just an old cheap piece that somebody had abandoned on a trash heap. Still, it was something he wanted, probably because it presented a nice problem in transportation. It tested his mettle. We first knew about his achievement when, deep in the night, we heard him trying to get the chest up onto the porch. It sounded as if two or three people were trying to tear the house down. We came downstairs and turned on the porch light. Rex was on the top step trying to pull the thing up, but it had caught somehow and he was just holding his own. I suppose he would have held his own till dawn if we hadn't helped him. The next day we carted the chest miles away and threw it out. If we had thrown it out in a near-by alley, he would have brought it home again, as a small token of his integrity in such matters. After all, he had been taught to carry heavy wooden objects about, and he was proud of his prowess.

I am glad Rex never saw a trained police dog jump. He was just an amateur jumper himself, but the most daring and tenacious I have ever seen. He would take on any fence we pointed out to him. Six feet was easy for him, and he could do eight by making a tremendous leap and hauling himself over finally by his paws, grunting and straining; but he lived and died without knowing that twelve- and sixteen-foot walls were too much for him. Frequently, after letting him try to go over one for a while, we would have to carry him home. He would never have given up trying.

There was in his world no such thing as the impossible. Even death couldn't beat him down. He died, it is true, but only as one of his admirers said, after "straight-arming the death angel" for more than an hour. Late one afternoon he wandered home, too slowly and too uncertainly to be the Rex that had trotted briskly homeward up our avenue for ten years. I think we all knew when he came through the gate that he was dying. He had apparently taken a terrible beating, probably from the owner of some dog that he had got into a fight with. His head and body were scarred. His heavy collar with the teeth marks of many a battle on it was awry; some of the big brass studs in it were sprung loose from the leather. He licked at our hands and, staggering, fell, but got up again. We could see that he was looking for someone. One of his three masters was not home. He did not get home for an hour. During that hour the bull terrier fought against death as he had fought against the cold, strong current of Alum Creek, as he had fought to climb twelve-foot walls. When the person he was waiting for did come through the gate, whistling, ceasing to whistle, Rex walked a few wobbly paces toward him, touched his hand with his muzzle, and fell down again. This time he didn't get up.

ONE

Gene Hill

I ADMIRED THE DOG out of courtesy and that was about it. He wasn't anything special to look at — just your nice, solid, big-headed black Lab. I've seen hundreds just like him, give or take an inch here or a detail there. His work in the field was efficient, but not exciting. He wasn't what a real fieldman would call steady and as often as not he'd drop a goose to readjust a hold; generally preferring to drag it along by a wing. He did have one peculiar habit I noticed — he never picked up a bird, no matter how dead it was without stepping on the neck with one foot first and holding it there until he'd grabbed the wing. I asked about this, and his owner told me that it was a habit he'd had from the first, since his first goose picked him pretty bad. This bit of cause and effect reasoning pleased me being a "once burned, twice shy" person myself.

This day in a goose pit on the eastern shore of Maryland

To ABSENT FRIENDS

was as common as the surrounding mud. Intermittent flights had us calling, more for the amusement of it than any real hope of turning them. But every so often a pair or a small flock of five or six would toll close enough for a shot and since we were in no hurry or that anxious to take geese, we took turns gunning. By mid-afternoon we each had two geese — enough for our personal satisfaction, but the weather was mild so we had come to a mutual unspoken agreement to just sit there and chat rather than pick up and go our separate ways. It was a lovely way to spend an afternoon — gunning talk mostly, a little fishing talk, some book titles exchanged — just your average small talk between two relative strangers who found common ground and an occasional bit of laughter that sweetened the conversation putting each of us at ease and wanting the other to find us good company... a small, pleasant spontaneous friendship.

He hardly mentioned his Lab, and neither did I, but I was pleased to notice that the dog sat leaning a little against his masters leg or put his head on his foot when he chose to lie down, and that my companions hand was stroking the dog or messing with his ears or scratching him behind the neck. It was just the sort of thing any one of us might do, an ordinary circumstance, a commonplace relationship. Nor did I find it strange that the dog paid absolutely no attention to me whatsoever. There are dogs that are nuisances for affection (several of mine were like that from being spoiled and encouraged to play) and others that like to keep to themselves, and others that are clearly one person creatures.

He had not bothered to bring a lunch, and I, for once,

had gotten myself together and packed one. As usual, when I do get the lunch-making urge, I tend to go overboard and had more than enough to share, which I gladly did. We each had two sandwiches, and as he ate his he fed the other to his dog at the same pace, bite for bite. A sandwich and a half was enough for me, so I offered the dog the half left over. He wouldn't touch it from my hand, so I placed it on the floor of the blind in front of him where it sat unnoticed and untasted until I asked my friend if the dog were on some sort of self-imposed diet.

"No, I don't think so," he laughed, and picked up the food and as before fed it to the dog bite by bite.

You can usually sense when someone has been waiting for a chance to talk about something that needs to be aired. You feel that he's been looking for the right time and place and ear. I was hoping that I'd have that privilege, so I just sat there and watched him dribble pieces of that sandwich, pieces about the size of 00 Buck, to a dog that was not only used to this little game, but so delighted with it that he was making soft moaning noises and rolling his eyes like a fundamentalist convert.

"Pete, here, is about the worst dog I've ever owned," he said with some hesitation, "but he's taught me more about dogs, in a strange way, than most of the others I've had — and there have been quite a few."

I just sat there and stared at the floor of the blind, not wanting to look at him, because he didn't want to look at me… right now he wanted a listener, a sympathetic and understanding one — one who had some knowledge of what he was talking about, but not a conversation — just the ear would do fine for the time being.

"If you've ever followed the big field trial circuit you'd probably know my name. For quite a few years I was the amateur trainer that most of the pro's worried about. And they had good reason. I had the money, the time, the drive and the dogs. And you needed all that just to start because you were in against the Belmonts, the Roosevelts, big steel money, big oil money and just plain money so big that hardly anyone remembered where it all had come from. One handler drove his dogs to the trails in an old Rolls Royce fitted up like a kennel truck; the people he worked for drove Rolls' and they didn't want their dogs in anything less! I didn't go that far... but I wasn't too far behind. I've charted more than one plane to take my dogs where I thought they ought to be running and I never regretted a penny of it.

"I even had Purdey make me a pair of side-bys just for field trial gunning in case my dogs didn't finish so I'd still be part of the action — and you learn a lot about certain dogs when you're a gun — but that's getting a little away from my story.

"It all started simply enough — and typically as far as I'm concerned. I've always loved competition — I've been a top flight amateur golfer, a tournament winner on the trap and skeet circuit, and got to where they knew I was there in the live bird rings of Madrid and Monte Carlo. Then I got to thinking about getting a dog. I traveled so much in my early days that owning one didn't make much sense. My hosts, when I went shooting, all had fine kennels so it didn't make any difference if I had any or not. In fact it was better that I didn't. But when a big holding company bought me out for more money than I could ever spend and moved me up to some spot that was all title and no work, I began to look around for something new to take up. It was just about destined that I'd start field trialing Labs.

"I'd been a member of one of those fancy Long Island duck clubs for years and had seen some pretty good dogs. It might sound silly, but I believe that a man has to have a dog and a breed of dog that suits his personality. If I believed in reincarnation I don't doubt that I'd come back as a Lab — or would like to. It's a little vain I know, but I saw myself as brave, honest and strong, as Hemingway might have put it, and that's what I like about the Lab. It's all up front, nothing held back.

"Anyway, one of my duck hunting buddies at the old Sprig Club had a litter of dogs out of good field trial stock and he gave me a male as sort of a retirement present. He said that at worst he'd be somebody I could talk to and take care of and get the same in return. After I'd spent a few weeks with the pup I decided to have a professional take a look at him. I felt that he might have what it would take to be a trial dog, but I believe in the opinions of the people who do it everyday, not just an amateur appraisal.

"The professional not only liked the dog but made an offer then and there to take him for training, and I agreed. He had a fine reputation and I liked his whole approach to the training idea. He was to start the dog, and when he was satisfied I'd come down and spend a week or so with him and learn to run the dog myself. Then I'd get a training schedule to work on and check back with him for a few days on a regular basis. If the dog did exceptionally well, he'd take him over completely and campaign in the major stakes. His name was Wonderdog — because I wondered what I'd do with him when I first got him; a little joke with myself. If you follow the retrievers you know how far he got and what a piece of pure bad luck it was he didn't become National Champion. He was killed a little while after his first Nationals — an assistant trainer was in an accident and the dog trailer was totally demolished. I was hurt by the loss, of course, but by then I'd been committed to try for another dog as good as he was. He'd sired a litter and I arranged to get the pick for stud service.

"If anything, he was better than his father; a bit more aggressive and strangely a bit more biddable. It was almost as if he felt destined to compete and understood what was expected of him all along. I called him Little Wonder — another private joke with myself. Almost everyone was soon calling him One, short for number one because that's what he looked like right from the start. He was one of the hottest derby dogs anyone had seen when he was right, and he usually was. I'd never thought of a dog as an athlete before One, but when he took to water he reminded me of a diver — I know it's silly to think of a dog having "form" but he did — and I never got over the idea that he knew it and worked at it.

"By the time he was three, One had totally captivated the trial circuit — not just in wins and placements, but by his personality — his pure competitiveness and genius for doing just the right thing at the right time. I know for sure that more than one judge laid out a series with just him in mind, but as hard as they tried to challenge him he was usually up to it. Of course he had an off-day now and then, disinterested or bored or maybe tired, but even then he did his job, but without the fire he was famous for. In his first National at Bombay Hook he placed third. I don't think he deserved to win, but I think he deserved at least second. The head judge and I weren't exactly friends, since I'd beaten his dog at several important trials and he wasn't above playing a little politics with some nationally known names.

"I'd planned to retire One after his first in the Nationals, and just use him as a stud dog and gunning companion. We'd become pretty close and I thought he deserved a little rest and some fun — and some of the fun had gone out of the competition as far as I was concerned. But I did want that win for him in the worst way. He'd worked hard for it and most of us still believed that he had the class and the talent to go all the way; if any dog deserved it, One certainly did. The more we worked him that season the sharper he got. I didn't think that there was much room for improvement, but in subtle ways he just looked better. His long blinds were precision itself and when he was stopped to the whistle he really *stopped*. It was as if he were reading your mind — I heard one judge remark in a friendly way that he looked as if he were showing off. I'm making him sound as if he were absolutely perfect, but he did have one small fault. Not in every trial, but every now and then for some reason he'd make one or two little yelps on a retrieve on land.

I always put it down as pure enthusiasm and the trainer and I had long given up trying to make him stop. More often than not, we'd be the only ones to notice it."

Here he paused for so long I didn't think he was going to go on with the rest of the story. He was rumpling his dog and searching for the right words and the strength to say them. I had the feeling that this was a story that he'd never told before and perhaps didn't want to — yet knew that he must so he could get a different grip on it himself. For some strange reason I thought of the words to an old song about "hanging your tears out to dry" — how perfectly put, how perfectly true.

For the first time since he'd begun, he turned to look at me and I could see the gray, sad sparkle of small tears. I turned away a bit to give him a moment of privacy. He covered his face with his handkerchief for just a second and went on.

"I'd say the chances of what happened ever happening are more than one in a million. One of those random tragedies that always seem to strike the innocent; the casual passerby. There was a strand of wire, just one, that was only about two feet long between an old post and a tree. I'd heard One making his odd yipping noise and suddenly he went end over end in the air and lay still. Both the judges and I rushed out knowing instantly that something fearful had happened, and there was One stretched out, dead from a broken neck. A small trickle of blood ran down the corners of his jaw where he'd run into the wire with his mouth open.

"I carried him back to the station wagon and put him on

the front seat and started to drive. I don't remember how long it was or where I went, but I do remember that I kept rubbing his head believing for the longest time that he'd suddenly sit up and everything would be all right. Today is the second time in my life that I've cried; that was the first.

"There's a small graveyard behind the lodge at the Sprig Club where our special dogs were put to rest and the whole club turned out to help me put him there. I had a blanket made of his ribbons and my gunning coat was his pillow. He always loved to sleep on that whenever he had the chance. One of the members read a list of his wins and when finished with that, he paused, and in a soft tenor began to sing Auld Lang Syne and everyone, except me, joined in with him."

He stopped again for a minute and blew his nose; I must confess I did the same.

"I virtually stopped gunning for a long time after that. When people asked me why, I told them that my favorite partner had passed away and almost none of them ever thought that it might have been just my dog. Funny, isn't it, how few can understand the relationship a man can have with his dog? And yet, I can tell you now that there were few, if any, things in my life that meant as much to me as One, and how odd but true that an emptiness like that is there forever.

"It's been about five years since I lost One and last fall a friend of mine, the same one that sang that afternoon at the duck club, came to my house and rang the bell. When I opened the door he reached in and put a puppy in my arms and said, 'It's about time Pete had someone to look after,' and turned and left."

"This is Pete." At the sound of his name Pete looked up and made some sort of a face that I'll say was as close to smiling as a dog can get.

"When I said that Pete was the worst of my dogs I didn't mean anything but that I'd never trained him. I just let him be Pete. And that's been enough, more than enough. They say that a man deserves one good dog in his life... but that's not true. I've had a couple, and in his own way, Pete's right there in my heart with them all now. It's a full space with two empty ones beside it if you can see it that way."

I nodded to let him know that I agreed, but I didn't say anything because I didn't think anything needed to be said just at that moment.

He began, after a little while, to talk about something else and after giving me his card he thanked me for listening and said it was time for him and Pete to be heading on home. I said goodbye and told him that I'd wait here a little while longer in the blind just to watch the sun come down. But that wasn't the whole truth. What I wanted to do was sit there in the quiet of twilight and hear the soft phrases of that ancient Scottish melody again in my mind and picture the scene of that group of men singing a dog to eternity and comforting themselves in the timeless ritual of shared sorrow and the understanding of loss.

In the last light, I slung my two geese over my shoulder and started back to where I'd left the car. I found myself softly singing what I could remember of One's funeral song, and surprisingly, I wasn't as saddened by the idea as you'd imagine. The saving thought was one of remembrance; as long as a man lives, so will his dogs in one form or another… in a story or a song. One will always be there to take care of the other and I can't think of a nicer way to put it than we will "share a cup of kindness now…"

WHERE TO BURY A DOG

Ben Hur Lampman

A SUBSCRIBER OF THE Ontario *Argus* has written to the
editor of that fine weekly, propounding a certain question,
which, so far as we know, remains unanswered. The question
is this: "Where shall I bury my dog?" It is asked in advance
of death. The *Oregonian* trusts the *Argus* will not be offended
if this newspaper undertakes an answer, for surely such a
question merits a reply, since the man who asked it, on the
evidence of his letter, loves the dog. It distresses him to think
of his favorite as dishonored in death, mere carrion in the
winter rains. Within that sloping, canine skull, he must
reflect when the dog is dead, were thoughts that dignified
the dog and honored the master. The hand of the master
and of the friend stroked often in affection this rough,
pathetic husk that was a dog.

We would say to the Ontario man that there are various
places in which a dog may be buried. We are thinking now

of a setter, whose coat was flame in the sunshine, and who, so far as we are aware, never entertained a mean or an unworthy thought. This setter is buried beneath a cherry tree, under four feet of garden loam, and at its proper season the cherry strews petals on the green lawn of his grave. Beneath a cherry tree, or an apple, or any flowering shrub of the garden, is an excellent place to bury a good dog. Beneath such trees, such shrubs, he slept in the drowsy summer, or gnawed at a flavorous bone, or lifted head to challenge some strange intruder. These are good places, in life or in death. Yet it is a small matter, and it touches sentiment more than anything else. For if the dog be well remembered, if sometimes he leaps through your dreams actual as in life, eyes kindling, questing, asking, laughing, begging, it matters not at all where that dog sleeps at long and at last. On a hill where the wind is unrebuked, and the trees are roaring, or beside a stream he knew in puppyhood, or somewhere in the flatness of a pasture land, where most exhilarating cattle graze. It is all one to the dog, and all one to you, and nothing is gained, and nothing lost — if memory lives. But there is one best place to bury a dog. One place that is best of all.

If you bury him in this spot, the secret of which you must already have, he will come to you when you call — come to you over the grim, dim frontiers of death, and down the well-remembered path, and to your side again. And though you call a dozen living dogs to heel they should not growl at him, nor resent his coming, for he is yours and he belongs there. People may scoff at you, who see no lightest blade of grass bent by his footfall, who hear no whimper pitched too fine for mere audition, people who may never really have had a dog. Smile at them then, for you shall know something that is hidden from them, and which is well worth the knowing. The one best place to bury a good dog, is in the heart of his master.

TO ABSENT FRIENDS

EPITAPH

Sir William Watson

HIS FRIENDS he loved. His direst earthly foes—
Cats — I believe he did but feign to hate.
My hand will miss the insinuated nose,
Mine eyes the tail that wagg'd contempt at fate.

THE LEGEND

Randy Wayne White

ONCE, VISITING THE Key West docks, I struck up a conversation with a shrimper, a true Conch, which is to say he
talked through his nose and wore white rubber boots. When
I told him where I lived — a coastal town more than 400
miles away by highway — he said, "Hey now, you ever heard
about that dog what they got up there?"

Dog?

"Yeah, that *there* dog. Dog can swim underwater and
bring up cement blocks. Whole ones, from 15 feet a water,
then swim them back to shore. Big brown curly lab. And
understands *words*. Say this dog can swim down fish; catch
them, too. Catches snook, reds; even a shark once. A friend
of mine was talking it around the docks. An ol' boy he knew
knows somebody what'd seen it. Man, I'd love to have one a
his pups."

The shrimper thought I might know something about
the stories, me being from the town where this dog was said

to live, and that led us into a discussion of other dogs; dogs that neither of us had really encountered, but had heard much about. The shrimper told me the story of the grouper boat cocker that had twice saved all hands: once by leading them to a fire in the dunnage box; another time by waking them when the anchor broke during a storm. Then he told me about the shrimp boat golden retriever that had dived overboard and drowned itself the trip after her owner was drowned. The golden, the shrimper told me, had a 200-word vocabulary and knew the days of the week. It was a great loss felt by all.

I had already heard both of these stories in various forms, and the shrimper had probably already heard my story about the feral hog that had killed 27 catch dogs but was finally brought down by a collie-rottweiler mix, and about the pit bull from LaBelle who would sink its teeth into moving truck tires and flop around and around until the truck stopped. All regions have their legendary dogs, and it has been my experience that outdoor people collect those stories, knowingly or not, perhaps because dogs, unlike people, are still safe harbors for exaggeration. We can tell the wildest tales about animals we have never met, absolutely fearless in the certainty that our wonder and our admiration will never be dashed by a "60 Minutes" exposé or Senate subcommittee hearings. That people are human is a reality now beyond escape; that dogs are not makes them, perhaps, the last stronghold of legend.

The shrimper wanted to know about the dog in my town; the dog that could retrieve cement blocks and outswim fish. The animal that understood *words*. But instead of telling the man the truth, I told him what he wanted to hear because, while I had not propagated the legend, I was, necessarily, through association and loyalty, another of its protectors. And I did know the truth. The dog he was describing was once my dog.

I called him Gator because that's the animal he most resembled while in the water, and, like the reptile, he possessed certain quirks of character not normally ascribed to creatures allowed outside a zoo, let alone welcomed into a house. He was not a lab, though I often hear him called that. He was a Chesapeake Bay retriever, seven months old when I got him from an Everglades hunting guide, and already the subject of dark rumors, though I did not know it at the time. A wealthy northern client had given him to the guide as a present, but the guide, who favored tall pointers and catch dogs, didn't know what to do with him. He kept him in a run with his pit bulls until the Chesapeake — then called Wolf because of his yellow eyes — opened the carotid artery of one of his prize bitches. The guide decided to try and sell the dog and, if that didn't work, he'd shoot the damn thing and burn the papers. All this, I heard later.

Coincidentally, I had recently ended an 11-year association with a nice setter and was casting around for a new breed to try. Most people who like dogs have some vague mental list of breeds they admire and, at that time, I was leaning toward border collies, flat-coated retrievers, or a nice mixed breed from the humane society. See, the difficulty in choosing a good dog now is that some of the great breeds have suffered at the hands of pet store puppy factories and certain lowlife bench show fanatics who have bred only for confirmation or cash flow, and I did not want one of their mindless, hyperactive progeny. It was then that I happened to read a newspaper article about a Chesapeake Bay retriever that had, according to eyewitnesses, leaped into a flooded creek and pulled out a drowning child.

I liked that.

I had one very young son with another on the way, and we lived on a creek. I began to research the breed — just as anyone contemplating dog ownership should. There were relatively few registered Chesapeakes in the country (little chance of overbreeding), and only the most generous of souls would describe them as pretty (of no interest to the puppy factories). Everything I read I liked so, after having the dog x-rayed for hip dysplasia, and after listening patiently while the guide insisted the dog had championship bloodlines (I've yet to see a registered dog that didn't), Gator ended up in my home.

Every dog I have ever owned learned the basic obedience commands — to sit, to stay, to heel, and to come — after about four weeks of short daily training sessions. Gator took twice that long, but once he learned something, it was as if it had been etched in stone — an appropriate metaphor, considering his intellect. The dog was no Mensa candidate, but the commands he did learn he carried out like a Marine. What I didn't have to teach him was how to get things out of the water. Water was to Gator what air is to birds. On land, he might lose himself in the mangroves (more than once) or run into walls (often), but water transformed him into a fluid being; a graceful creature on a transcendent mission. The mission was simple: There were things in the creek — *many things* — that needed to be brought out. Our backyard became a littered mess of barnacled branches, shells, and other flotsam, even though each exit from the creek required that he latch his paws over the lip of a stone wall and then haul himself over, an exercise much like a pull-up. Since the dog did these pull-ups hundreds of times a day, month after month, his chest and forearms, quite naturally, became massive. Freakishly large. And, as the dog grew, so did the size of the things he retrieved. Tree branches became whole tree limbs. Shells became rocks — big rocks — for the dog learned early on that if the creek's surface was sometimes bare, the creek's bottom always held treasure. On a flood tide, the water was 7-feet deep and murky, but it made no difference. He would dive down and hunt and hunt until I thought surely a real gator had taken him, only to reappear 20 yards away, a rock or a limb in his mouth.

One morning I was sitting on the stoop reading when I noticed a neighbor's Boston Whaler drifting pilotless toward our property. I thought this odd until I realized my dog was towing it home. He had chewed the lines free with his teeth, and an emergency survey of other mooring lines in the area provided strong evidence that, had I accepted the Whaler, a 30-foot Chris Craft would soon follow.

At some juncture during that era of boat thievery, four more things occurred that enhanced his already growing reputation in the region: He dove underwater and retrieved his first cement block, he caught his first fish, he jumped through a second-story window to attack a pit bull, and he got an ear infection. Swimming the block ashore didn't surprise me, though the stranger who had come asking to see the dog and then threw the block seemed genuinely shocked. Catching the fish did surprise me, because I had watched Gator sit on the dock studying waking fish, only to dive and miss them year after year. Finally, though, he did manage to stun and swim one down, and he brought it to me, his tail wagging mildly (a mad display of emotion for that dog); a 10-pound jack crevalle that swam strongly away when I released it. The ear infection was a more subtle touch. It required an operation that left the dog's head listing slightly to the left, and people who came to see him would say things like, "See there? He knows we're talking about him, and he's trying to understand," for the tilt did lend an air of rakish intellect to an otherwise blank expression.

Added to all of this were Gators all-too-often public displays of his own dark nature. Spending his earnest months in a run with pit bulls had left him with a mean-spirited view of dogs in general and of pit bulls in particular. I could take him jogging on free heel, and he never looked at another dog. But if one strayed onto the property, bad things happened. We were moving into a new stilthouse when a big pit bull came trotting into the yard, giving great ceremony to the decision of where to pee. I had been warned about this dog. He had free rein of the neighborhood, terrorizing pets and children, and the owners would do nothing. Gator was on the upstairs porch, watching with me through the screened window… and then, suddenly, he was no longer there. It took me a long dull moment to understand what had happened, looking through the broken screen as Gator, making an odd chirping sound because the fall had knocked the wind out of him, attacked the pit bull. Gator accompanied the pit bull home, which is where the pit bull stayed — once his stitches were removed and he was released from the animal hospital.

I consider what my Chesapeake did that afternoon less an act of bravery than just one more demonstration that certain basic concepts — the effects of gravity, for instance — were utterly beyond him. I don't doubt for a moment that he would have dived into a flooded creek to pull out a drowning child. But he would have gone in just as quickly to rescue a log or a Subaru. We love to attribute to animals those noble qualities we lack, though often long for, in ourselves. But Gator wasn't noble; he was only pure of purpose. Other dogs suffered unhappy encounters with him. A few deserving people suffered too.

Once a burly lawman I did not know arrived at the house in a van. With the barest of introductions, the lawman told me loudly that he did not believe the stories he'd heard about my dog, but he'd come to see for himself. Then, as if to underline his contempt for exaggeration, he slid open the van's side door and two big Doberman pinschers jumped out — inexcusable behavior on the lawman's part, but that's exactly what he did.

Gator was in the creek tearing out mangroves when he windscented the Dobermans, and he came charging over the bank, blowing water from his nose and roaring; roaring because that was the only noise he could make with a tree limb in his mouth. The Dobermans were too stunned by this draconic vision to move and so fared badly in Gator's attack from the sea. The lawman could move, but moving was exactly the wrong thing to do, which is why Gator turned his attention to the lawman, who was trying feverishly to drag his two dogs back into the van. The lawman left, making threats out the van window. My dog had bitten him, and also injured two trained police dogs. I would hear from the authorities, he promised. And he kept his promise.

The next day, a squad car pulled into the drive followed by a van from animal control. They wanted to see my dog. I whistled for Gator, and he came trotting around the corner carrying, to my surprise, a 20-pound hammerhead I had been dissecting on the dock. From inside the animal control van, I heard one of the men say, "Holy Lord, he kills sharks, too. I'm not getting out."

But the men did get out. They watched Gator retrieve bird dummies. They watched him retrieve the cement block. They saw how he worked on hand signals. And when Gator had finished doing all this, one of the men said, "See how he tilts his head when we talk? It's like he understands what we're saying. Man, I'd love to have one a this dog's pups."

Gator's reputation spread.

Television stations sometimes called to see if I would allow them to do a piece on Gator (always refused) just as the friends of friends sometimes stopped to watch the dog who swam underwater and caught sharks. More than once, in those years, I heard a stranger describe my own dog to me with details as wondrous as they were exaggerated.

But, in reality, Gator was probably not much different from dogs you have known or owned. He was a good dog, which is to say he minded well, and he was mine. When I got up to leave the room, he followed. He was good with the boys, didn't yap, didn't hump, didn't whine, didn't eat the furniture, didn't jump up on strangers unless he meant to bite them, only stole the one boat unless you count canoes, and he wouldn't have gone for the cavalry if I had waited a year.

He wasn't an overly affectionate dog, either. He liked to have his ears scratched, but I can remember only one time in our nine years that he actually licked me. I had given up hunting because I simply took no joy anymore in killing for sport those same animals I loved to watch while on the water or in the field. But I had made that decision, I saw now, without giving any thought to the dog I had trained exactly for that purpose. I had, I realized too late, defected, in a small way, to the ranks of bad breeders and bench show fanatics by robbing another working dog of its heritage.

So I decided to give hunting one more try. I loaded Gator and shotgun into the boat and ran the tidal creek to a saw-grass marsh where, I knew, there were brackish ponds that held scaup and mallards. It would have been a bad day for fishing anyway, but it was a fine day for ducks: February gray and windy, with sea fog over the bay. Gator felt good, I could tell. He kept his ears perked like a puppy, and his yellow eyes glowed, and I wondered, *How can he know?*

It had been years since we had hunted together. But now,

as then, he understood that this was not just a boat ride. This was not playtime. Cement blocks and sunken logs were meaningless; swimming before a shot was fired, unforgivable. This, he knew, was *work*.

I positioned him at the water's edge, but close enough so that my left hand could reach his ears, and we waited. I missed two easy shots before I finally took a single — a mallard drake — and Gator vibrated beneath my hand, listening for the release, *Bird!*, before sliding into the water, throwing a wake in the dark chop as he found the mallard and pivoted as if equipped with a keel. I watched him swimming toward me, that big brown tilted head and those eyes. He should have brought the bird to my feet and then sat, but he didn't. He couldn't. His hips were ruined by disease, and he licked my hand as I scooped him up, telling me that it hurt when I held him that way, but there was only one alternative, and that would soon come.

I carried Gator back to the boat and placed him on the deck by my feet. Then I drove the legend homeward, toward his rendezvous with 9 ccs of pentobarbital, and the grave I had already dug for him.

To Boatswain

Lord Byron built a monument to his beloved
Newfoundland dog, Boatswain, in the garden of his
family home. First came an inscription, then the poem.

Near this spot
Are deposited the Remains
of one
Who possessed Beauty
Without Vanity,
Strength without Insolence,
Courage without Ferocity,
And all the Virtues of Man
Without his Vices.

This Praise, which would be unmeaning flattery
If inscribed over Human Ashes,
Is but a just tribute to the Memory of
'Boatswain', a Dog
Who was born at Newfoundland
May, 1803,
And died at Newstead Abbey
Nov. 18,1808.

TO BOATSWAIN

When some proud son of man returns to earth,
Unknown to glory, but upheld by birth,
The sculptor's art exhausts the pomp of woe,
And storied urns record who rests below;
When all is done, upon the tombs is seen,
Not what he was, but what he should have been:
But the poor dog, in life the firmest friend,
The first to welcome, foremost to defend,
Whose honest heart is still his master's own,
Who labours, fights, lives, breathes for him alone,
Unhonoured falls, unnoticed all his worth,
Denied in heaven the soul he held on earth;
While man, vain insect! hopes to be forgiven,
And claims himself a sole, exclusive heaven.
O man! thou feeble tenant of an hour,
Debased by slavery, or corrupt by power,
Who knows thee well must quit thee with disgust,
Degraded mass of animated dust!
Thy love is lust, thy friendship all a cheat,
Thy smiles hypocrisy, thy words deceit!
By nature vile, ennobled but by name,
Each kindred brute might bid thee blush for shame.
Ye! who, perchance, behold this simple urn,
Pass on – it honours none you wish to mourn:
To mark a friend's remains these stones arise:
I never knew but one, and here he lies.

TIPPY

Gene Hill

SOMEONE SAID THAT THE ONLY place you can bury a dog is in your heart. That way you can call the dog in for a little chat now and then — teasing it about being a clumsy puppy and looking down at your old hunting boots remembering who it was that put the teeth marks in them. You can hunt a day or so again, together, when you need a certain kind of memory — another day you like better than the one you're living in right now.

There's a big hole under the swamp maple in the front yard that Tippy dug, to nap away hot summer afternoons in the coolness of the dirt; and another one under the dogwood that she would fill with leaves that she liked for warmth and when the weather turned around — she'd come into the house smelling like November.

She was always a lady in the old-fashioned sense; quiet, well-mannered and gentle with an overwhelming fondness for little babies. She was always poking her nose into a crib or a playpen or stroller, seemingly immune to being poked in the eye or having her ears tugged — maybe because she slept with my daughter Patty in the days when they were both puppies.

I might be wrong, but I really don't remember losing a bird that I shot over Tip. She was a marvelous dog to watch in a field trial or from a duckblind. She was an exciting marker on a downed game, rock steady to shot, and when she entered the water you knew she was determined to leap as far as she could — she had style and pride and you could feel it. I'm sure she knew it pleased me to show her off a little in hunting camp.

And she was just as fine on upland game. I'd say "Tip, why don't you get in and hunt that thicket for me. I'll bet there's a bird in there." In she'd go and I'd always marvel how she'd mark a pheasant or a woodcock from a spot so dense. You wouldn't think she could see a flying bird, but she'd be right about where it went a lot more than I was.

It's not really important that Tip was a good dog to hunt over, but it is important to me that she was a good dog to be with. She was my pal. We enjoyed being with each other. I don't know that you can ask for much more.

I don't want you to think that I'm bragging her up. I just want to tell you a little bit about her because you weren't ever able to meet her and now the time has passed. Most of us have had one dog or so that we'd have liked friends to enjoy — and Tip was mine.

It always seems wrong to me that a man's life is so out of

phase with his dog's. You ought to be able to enjoy your youth together and grow old together. Fourteen years wasn't enough time for me to live with Tip. I wasn't even ready to admit to myself that she was getting on… when she was gone.

But somehow you learn to live with these things and discover, happily, that a man's ability to care deeply about dogs is without limit. He has room in his heart for them all. Tippy's daughter and granddaughter sleep by my feet and walk with me and get mad when they can't go out with me — just the way Tippy did. And I strongly suspect that before too long there will be a great granddaughter tumbling around chasing the cat, adding a new set of tooth marks on my hunting boots and getting up on the good furniture — another Tippy, to be sure, knowing that there's always enough love left for one more.

One day soon, on the swamp maple above the dusting hole, I'm going to put a small brass plate with the word TIPPY on it. And there will only be one of those.

WRINKLE AND I

Ross Santee

THE PUP WAS ASLEEP. His warm bed was in a shallow box behind the kitchen stove, beside the box was a pan of clean ashes for the puppy's needs. While Mother was always a gentle person, she could be firm; when Mother housebroke a puppy or kitten there was no piddling or puddling about the house. And the pup was a surprise.

Of course, I could hold him for he was mine. He grunted, still half asleep, when I picked him up. He didn't smell like a kitten when I held him against my neck; Mother said puppies had a smell of their own the same as kittens. And what would I call him? I didn't know, but he looked kind of wrinkled to me. "That might be a good name," suggested Mother, "if it pleases you." And so we called him Wrinkle.

I was not allowed to hold him when I ate, but he was asleep in my arms when the second bell rang for school.

"Now, heel it, son," Mother said, "or you'll be late. He'll be here when you get home."

At recess I told Bert Phillips about him, Bert was my first friend. When school let out Bert and 1 raced all the way. Wrinkle was asleep, but I carried him outside and put him down on the wooden sidewalk. Like all pups he spraddled out for it was a big, strange and new world to him but he did his best to please. When I spoke he tried to come to me; he finally took a header off the walk that was all of eight inches high and landed in a pile of autumn leaves. I picked him up and let Bert hold him, and my friend agreed that he was the finest pup that ever lived.

Someone suggested that if I wanted to make a good "ratter" out of him that I put the pup in a box with a rat and let them have it out. I was too small to realize how cruel it was, but it seemed like a good idea at the time. The wire trap in the corn crib at the barn often held more than a dozen sizable rats when I inspected it in the morning. One of the first chores that I recall was dumping the trap into a half barrel of water and dispatching the vermin that way.

I took a large tight packing box from the kindling yard, one deep enough that I didn't think a rat could scale the sides. But as a precaution I kept a broomstick handy. After taking such precautions I put Wrinkle in with him. He was still a puppy, still had his puppy teeth, and not much bigger than the rat he had been called to do battle with. Wrinkle knew it wasn't another puppy or a kitten, but he was perfectly willing to play.

It wasn't until the rat bit him and the puppy squealed that I realized what a cruel thing I'd done. I couldn't use the broomstick for fear of hitting the pup. And he was a fuzzy ball of fury now. Aside from the first squeal, the only sound the puppy made was a little throaty growl; it was the rat that did the squealing as they raged about the box. Wrinkle knew the fight was to the death and he was game to the core.

Mother finally heard me crying and cussing from the house, and knowing I was in trouble she appeared upon the scene. For I was in the box with them when Wrinkle laid him low. Even with the dead rat he still raged like a little fury. It was Mother who picked him out of the box and examined the puppy's wounds. "Of course, you didn't know any better," she said, "but you won't do it again. What a gritty little fellow he is." It wasn't until we reached the house that Mother discovered the rat had also bitten me. But Mother not only had a green thumb when it came to growing things, her hands were healing too.

He grew into a clean-bodied, clean-legged black and tan terrier and we were inseparable. When he was big enough to follow he was always at my heels. Older boys and grown men too thought it amusing the way he'd snap and bite when they made a pass at me. But it wasn't so amusing when he lost his puppy teeth. And while he tolerated the neighbors he was never a friendly dog, and the sight of a stranger passing our house would always touch him off.

We had gone uptown on an errand for Mother. There was a group of men at the hitching rack at Seymour's

General Store. We were passing the rack when the stranger spoke, a farm hand I'd never seen before. "There's that feist that run out an' bit me when I passed the house." As he spoke, the man pulled up his overalls. He wore no socks. It was obvious that he had come from the fields for his leg was dirty. The teeth marks were obvious too.

Now a small boy might take a personal insult from a grown man but it is always advisable to let his dog alone. "He's not a feist." I said, "for he's my dog." In the meantime Wrinkle, thinking it was the usual game, planted himself firmly between us, emitting throaty growls the while and showing his fine strong teeth.

The farm hand spoke again. "You're feisty, too, for so small a brat." As he spoke he aimed a kick at the dog. But it was an old game to Wrinkle and the little dog was quick. In the hassle that followed the farm hand was bitten again. Wrinkle and I both heeled it then. And on our return from our errand, as a matter of discretion, we passed the rack on the opposite side of the street.

We hunted rabbits that winter without success for we were both pretty small. When the snow was deep I carried him. Armed with a broomstick the pup and I worked every brush pile we could find. As for our winter's hunting we had more success at the barns for a rat was Wrinkle's mortal enemy until the day he died. And while Iowa boasted of its corn, it was rat-heaven for the vermin.

At the word "rats" Wrinkle would go into a tizzy. Mother finally forbade me saying the word in the house for at any mention of the word he would take the place apart. In bad weather we spent hours at the barns together; while I prodded and poked in odd places with the broomstick, Wrinkle dispatched the vermin when they came into the open. The hands at Lucas' farm next door often helped with the aid of a three-tined fork.

Dan Lucas, a neighbor, had holdings in the Northwest. It was not unusual for a trainload of Longhorns to be unloaded in our little town and the cowhands who accompanied them often wintered next door. They were eager participants too in what they called the "rat killin'" that we held most every morning. And like most cowhands I have known, a wager no matter how small was meat and drink to them.

For no longer did I dump the rat trap in the half barrel of water; the extermination of the vermin fell to Wrinkle, and how he enjoyed that chore. As long as one rat was dumped from the trap at a time I would wager a penny that no vermin could escape. Nor do I recall ever losing. But occasionally the hands made bets among themselves. When several rats were released from the trap at once some were bound to escape for Wrinkle never turned one loose until he was as dead as the proverbial door nail.

And of all Lucas' hands that I recall two are long-remembered. It could be the fact that they treated me as an equal and neither ever teased me nor did they tease my dog. One was John Scott and the other was Bert Morrison. Mother let me go any place with them.

John had gone to the pond to cut ice so the steers could water out. It was during the Xmas holidays and zero weather.

Mother had bundled me so tight I had trouble moving about. I carried the pup in my arms. We were ready to leave when a big steer got on the prod. When he charged the empty rack I held on to the pup as best I could for I thought we were going over.

"Take it easy," said John, "if he tries it again I'll drop him." John had a .44 Winchester in the rack. He pumped a shell into the barrel and when the big steer charged the rack the second time John not only dropped him in his tracks, he got down and butchered the critter. He gave me the bladder as a souvenir and blew it up for me.

But it was too cold to play outside. After I'd kicked it about in the house for a time the bladder finally disappeared, and I always suspected Mother.

Bert Morrison was a cowboy. Years later when I read "The Virginian," that character — the tall black-headed guy — to me was always Bert. Wrinkle and I were always at his heels when he was on the ground. And the "long" rides to the Lucas' feed barns to the south and west were special occasions for the barns were more than a half mile from town. I'd gather Wrinkle in my arms, then Bert would swing me up in front. Nor was he ever one to ask a pony's permission as to whether he liked it or not.

There was one ride I recall where Wrinkle got all the worst of it. I had him in my arms when Bert swung me up in front. The pony went to pitching then and somewhere along the line I dropped my pup. That ride was rough; at times I dangled most precariously, but Bert still held me in an ample paw when the pony's head came up. I was afraid the pony might kick the pup if he tried to follow and the idea of leaving Wrinkle behind was the last thing on my mind. Bert was agreeable; when he swung me up in front the second time I managed to hold the pup, and with Bert holding me we finally rode out the storm.

My friends and I occasionally tried damming up the creek as a swimming pool, but seldom with any success; the dam usually went out on us before the water was belly-deep. It was much simpler to go to the railroad pond on the other side of town, and while the pond was off limits for me I learned to swim that summer.

There were usually older boys at the pond who took delight in throwing small fry into deep water, wetting clothes and tying them in knots. Since Wrinkle always guarded my clothes I was seldom molested. At any movement toward me there was usually a warning shouted, "You better lay off that one unless you want to get dog-bit!"

It was late summer. We had moved Wrinkle's bed out on the porch where he always waited for me when I opened the kitchen door. Then the morning came when he couldn't get out of his bed. Mother was afraid it was poison. I had never heard of a veterinary for there was none in our little town, but I ran for Dr. Hamilton, the family physician. His team and buggy was at the rack; he was just ready to make some early calls in the country when I barged into his office above the general store.

"What is it, Lengthy?" he said.

"Doctor, my dog is sick. He's awful sick."

The doctor spoke in his quiet voice, "We'll go and look at him right now."

We went to the house where he examined the dog. It was poison, he said, and since Mother had already done the right things there was nothing more he could do. When I searched his face for a ray of hope the doctor shook his head. "No, Lengthy," he said, "he's a pretty sick little dog."

I was shocked when Mother apologized for me fetching him — Wrinkle was as much a part of the family to me as my mother and sisters. And I recall the good doctor's reply. "It's quite all right; I understand how Lengthy feels for after all I have three boys of my own."

The days dragged on and they were interminable. I sat by the bed on the porch. Mother sent me on long errands of no point that I could see; instead of dawdling as was my usual custom I ran the errands both ways. Mother was hopeful too. When she finally insisted I go to bed that night I thought he might pull through.

It was breaking light next morning when I went to his bed on the porch. At first glance he might have been asleep as he often slept on his back — then I saw the distorted face. Mother dressed and hurried out when she heard me crying and cussing, for I knew all the barnyard words. And Mother was shocked when I said that as soon as I got big enough I'd kill whoever did it.

"Don't say such things!" she said. "Don't even think such things." Mother covered him with one of his blankets. She spoke of my father who had died when I was only a few months old. "You were too small to remember him. This is your first real hurt."

I dug the grave by an apple tree under Mother's supervision and got by pretty well until Mother carried him from his bed wrapped in his little blanket. I heeled it then for the big ragweed thicket by the slaughter house. Wrinkle and I always went there when I wanted to be alone. It was hours later when I returned. Nor did Mother insist that I eat, she understood why I went to bed without supper that night.

The dog had bitten many people, yet there were only two suspects as far as I was concerned. One was the big lout who had threatened to cut off my ample ears, the other was the farm hand. When I asked my friend Bert Morrison to shoot either one or both men for me Bert was almost as shocked as Mother. "Listen, kid," he said, "you can't go around shootin' folks whether they need it or not. But if I find out who did it I'll work him over for you."

Since my friend Bert had let me down I took things in hand myself. But when I faced the big lout I didn't get far with him; he not only stoutly denied it, he called me a "damn little wild cat."

The farm hand was at the rack by the hardware store with a group of men days later when I finally located him. I was crying when I faced him but they were tears of rage. "You killed my dog — you poisoned him — and I hope the lightning strikes you!"

The farm hand slowly shook his head and his were kindly eyes. "No, kid," he said. "He bit me; fact is, he bit me twicet. I tried to kick him too, but I wouldn't do a lousy thing like that. I lost the first dog I ever owned that way, somebody poisoned him. I'm sorry about your little dog for I know how you feel."

I was always somewhat dubious about the big lout; but as for the farm hand with the kindly eyes, I knew he spoke the truth.

LAST RUN

Gary Paulsen

THE STORM WAS WILD, torn from the belly of the Arctic
north by two-hundred-mile-an-hour jet-stream winds and
dumped down on Minnesota like a scourge. Trees were
frozen and exploded when they could not contain the
expanding moisture within, the wind snapping them away
like straw. Cattle were found dead, deer frozen stiff, horses
and moose killed, and people, always some people caught
out in it to lose fingers and toes and ears and, for those who
were drunk, to die, frozen in a ditch or in their car only ten,
fifteen, twenty yards from the house. One young woman is
found frozen so solid they cannot get a needle into her arm
and somehow, in some miracle nobody understands, she lives
with only a finger gone while a mile away a man dies in his
car, warm as toast, from carbon monoxide that leaks up
through the floor because he is drunk and doesn't know
enough to clear away the snow.

Cookie and I sit in the living room watching television. These things have happened:

On a run not too long in the past Cookie started to limp. I rubbed her feet and looked for cuts and even used a magnifying glass and could find nothing, but the limp persisted. She favored both back legs. I gave it four days without running and when it didn't go away, worrying, I took her to the veterinarian.

He tested and retested and took X-rays and came out of the room and shook his head.

"What is it?" I asked.

"Arthritis. She has a mild case in her back ankles. She'll be fine if you don't run her."

Don't run her? We had so many miles together, so many rivers and lakes and hills and mountains — she had led for a whole Iditarod, all the way to Nome from Anchorage. I couldn't imagine not looking up and seeing Cookie.

"Are you sure?" I asked.

He nodded and held up the X-ray. "See here, at the ankle? See this swelling? You'll have to retire her, use another leader."

I sighed and nodded. "I have some others but I've always run her..."

"Not anymore."

And so she retired. It was not easy. I took her out of the kennel and moved her to the house. She had been in the house on only one occasion, when she ate an entire box of Cheerios, swallowing it nearly whole, a partial roast on *top* of the refrigerator, a full pound of butter in one gulp, and had a leather glove with meat smell on it halfway down her throat when I finally got her outside.

It took some time to get her adjusted to the newness and temperature. I took her around the yard, introduced her to the chickens (those that had miraculously lived past the puppies), one yard cat, though I couldn't find the other, and then I brought her in the house, where I gave her an introduction to Tudor. This did not go well and Cookie wore the scars of the introduction for the rest of her life, although an uneasy truce was held from then on.

I made an initial mistake by thinking generically. I assumed it was all right to show Cookie one cat and tell her "NO!" in a stern voice and she would understand that meant for all cats, the same with chickens and house dogs. I was wrong. Cookie was more specific and the next morning the cat I had not introduced her to was gone. We looked for it for a day and more until I saw a pile of Cookie's stool with the cat's collar in it and knew what had happened. After that I made certain to show her each and every thing she was not supposed to do.

We had by this time accumulated quite a menagerie other than the sled dogs. We loved dogs in general and people knew this, and almost any dog that was not wanted found its way (often mysteriously left at our door) to our home. We had a small terrier, a Chihuahua, a Border collie, a half-Lab, a rottweiler, a non-descript farm breed, and a small yellow mutt. Cookie had to meet each of them, understand that each of them was protected and allowed to live in the same house. Once she figured it all out, she moved in.

It was still not without some difficulty. Cookie had always been the number-one dog and knew it. When she came into the house she "marked" (peed) in the corner of each room to establish her territory, which did not exactly endear her to Ruth. But after some time Cookie learned she could only mark in one spot and I kept a paper there that I threw out immediately afterward.

"It's this way," Ruth said when it all seemed to be settling down. "As long as everybody — and I do mean *everybody* — does exactly as she tells them to do at every moment of every day and every night it will be all right."

"That's how I see it," I said, watching Cookie walk through the kitchen and make Tudor hit the top of the refrigerator and stick to the ceiling. "Pretty much."

"Well, good then," she said, nodding. "Just so I know…"

I went ahead and ran dogs with other leaders, trained for what I hoped would be my next Iditarod. Cookie had some trouble when she heard me harnessing for those first few runs. Ruth said she nearly tore the house apart trying to get out the first time. But Ruth gave her bits of meat and other treats — she had developed a taste for peanut brittle, which we made often — and after the fourth or fifth run, when she heard me harnessing she just trotted into the kitchen to get a piece of pea-nut brittle from Ruth and went back to her cedar-shavings bed.

The training went well, or seemed to, but after a few months I climbed into the middle of one whale of a fight between Minto and William, who had both fallen in love with Frenchy, a little Canadian female given to me by a trapper.

I grabbed each of them and pulled them apart. They fought to get back at each other and I pulled harder and felt a sudden pain in my chest. I had once ripped my sternum loose and I thought that's what had happened.

The pain went away, but a week later I had to fly to Boston on business and in the Boston airport for no apparent reason the same pain came back and this time I knew what it was. The tests proved positive. I had heart disease, and the doctor told me almost the exact thing the vet had told me about Cookie.

"You'll have to hang it up and not run the dogs anymore..."

And so I retired with Cookie. Initially I had the idea that my life would be sedate. I found someone to take the dogs (and he is still running them) and I moved into the house. I mistakenly thought I would have to sit a lot, and for the first time in eight years I bought a television set and a satellite dish to help pass what I thought would be monotonous hours. The truth was I couldn't watch it. I tried. I would sit on the couch and turn the thing on in the evening and Cookie would come and sit next to me — she *loved* it and kept trying to look in back of the set and see where the people were — and we would try to watch it together. I had come to know greater things in my life, however, and television had become so appallingly awful that I simply couldn't watch it (and still can't).

So I sat and wrote notes in longhand with an old fountain pen for books I hoped to write, while Cookie watched, growling if somebody came to sit too close to me and lifting her lip if a dog or cat appeared on the screen. The months passed and we evolved from friends who had run thousands of miles together to friends who would sit and talk together. She stayed with me constantly, wherever I went in the house. Even the bathroom. If I locked her out of a room she tore at the door until I would open it, then she would come in and sit near me — eating, resting, bathing. Wherever. If I went outside she followed, each time I left, even for an armload of wood. When I sat and read — which I did more and more — she would sit nearby, or lie down and half sleep, one ear cocked to hear if I moved or said anything. And so we spent our days and I thought we would continue to spend them.

It had been months since I'd let the dogs go and some of the grieving at losing the kennel and team had abated, or the edges had dulled.

I assumed the same had happened to Cookie. She seemed to love lying around watching television, walking with me to the mailbox to get the mail — a daily event — and sitting on the back porch and watching the loons come back from whatever mysterious southern world they go to in the winter. Summer passed and the grass grew back where the kennel had been and a neighbor farmer plowed and disked and planted alfalfa where the pups had run. By early fall, when the alfalfa was knee-high, the last signs of the kennel were obliterated and visually, at least, it seemed there had never been the noise and joy of the dogs.

But for two things...

There came the first hard fall morning. I arose early — the diet and exercise and medication had helped and I was becoming more active; not as I had been but better all the time — and I went out for wood for the stoves. Cookie, of course, went with me. She had slept next to my side of the bed, arose with me, and followed me into the bathroom and watched while I brushed my teeth and dressed and then, of course, followed me outside.

The fall color was in full bloom and the oaks and maples and poplars around the house and the field looked like a garish impressionist painting. To say it was beautiful was an understatement — it was very nearly in poor taste, the colors so loud and vivid they cut the eyes, went into the mind.

There was, for the first time in the year, a snap to the weather. Not bitter cold but just that, a snap, enough to sting the cheeks and ears and fingers. I walked to the woodpile to split kindling for the wood-stove and Cookie accompanied me. But at the pile I stopped and she kept going.

Out, into the field, to where the kennel had been. I watched her go and knew what she was thinking. First long runs came with first cold, the first real reaches, and Cookie used to love them, loved to take off when there was not always the possibility of coming home. I called her but she ignored me and kept going, and I put the ax down and followed her out into the drying alfalfa stubble. There was, literally, no sign there'd ever been a dog there, let alone seventy or eighty of them. The neighbor had plowed and eradicated any indication, but Cookie knew exactly where everything had been. She went to the precise spot where she'd stood so many hundreds, perhaps thousands, of times, where she had waited in harness for the rest of the dogs to be harnessed and hooked up, and looked back as if expecting dogs to be there, ready for the first long run, the beginning of fall.

"No," I said, coming up next to her. "There aren't any."

She looked up at me, then back to the rear, and whined softly.

"We don't do that now. Come, come with me back to the woodpile."

I walked off and beckoned but she hung back, stayed for another thirty or forty seconds, a minute — it seemed an hour — and I would have gone back to coax her but I would have lost it. It took everything in me to keep walking and not look back at her standing there waiting, and when at last she caught up with me, still whining, I reached down to pet her and she leaned in against my leg.

I thought that was the last time the memory would bother her but I was wrong. There was to be one more time. She would rise one more time, and it came during a storm.

Fall had surrendered to winter not with a blast but with a whimper, easing in to soft rain and low gray days, turning gradually to slushy snow and never the clean, hard brittle beauty that was northern winter.

Until the storm.

We were secure. The house was tight, there were sixteen cords of oak cut and split nearby, the chimneys were clean, the pantry full of good — vegetarian — food. Even Tudor, normally upset by weather, had settled in for winter and sat on the back of the couch, one eye warily on Cookie because he still didn't trust her, staring out at the wind ravaging the trees and driving snow sideways.

Cookie asked to go out. She had become — except for marking her paper daily — the model of cleanliness and was housebroken to a fault, and she went to the window and put her feet up on the sill and whined and looked out and then moved to the door, and without thinking I let her out.

But it was not because she had to go to the bathroom. Not this time.

We had always run to storms. I am not certain how it started but at some point early on in our training, either consciously or subconsciously, I had decided that the worse the weather, the better it was for training. In a way it made sense because nothing in Minnesota — not the very worst storms I have ever seen — could prepare us for the storms and winds in the interior of Alaska, where I have seen people literally blown off their sleds and cartwheeling out across the tundra. But the upshot of this all was that whenever it got bad we ran, and Cookie had learned this as a pattern and I had forgotten it.

When I let her out I always watched because her arthritis was acting up and she had trouble walking. I expected her to hit the yard, get her business done, and come back in the house. But she didn't do anything I expected. Instead she smelled the wind, stood for a moment, wheeled and headed back for what used to be the kennel.

"Darn," I said.

"What?" Ruth was by the stove with a cup of coffee.

"I have to go out . . ."

"In this?"

I found my parka and, bundled with the hood up and

tied, staggered out into the wind and into the open field, where the gusts almost blew me over. The snow was new and nearly a foot deep but Cookie's tracks were already filled in. It didn't matter because I knew where she was going and had been there so many times I didn't need to see the direction.

I found her in the same place, standing alone in the kennel in the harnessing position, waiting, the wind tearing at her, her nose up and into the storm, smelling, knowing what we had to do, waiting for me to harness her and the dogs.

I stood next to her and petted her neck and held her there while the wind and storm came at us and she whined, a soft sound barely over the howl of wind, and I shook my head so she could see it.

"No," I said. "It's done now, it's all over — no more runs."

And that time she understood. She leaned against my leg as she had done so many times so I could pet her head and the whine ended then, for the last time the whine to run, the beg to run, and I started back for the house and she walked with me and didn't need to be convinced.

Two more summers and one more winter went by while I kept to my diet and somehow got better and Cookie took the yard, owned it, and owned the house and became part of my new life as she had once been part of the old, of the runs, the long runs.

And then one morning, a soft morning in late summer, I let her out and she did not come back in for breakfast, to be with me, to be close to me. After a cup of tea I went into the yard and called her. It was the first time in those

To Absent Friends

years since I had been home that she had not been with me for any length of time, and when she did not come to my call I knew, I think, but I looked anyway. I found her under the spruce tree, her face to the east, dead with her eyes half open.

I sat for a time next to her, crying for her and mostly in self-pity because I would have to live without her now, and then I took her back to the place in the kennel where she loved to stand, the place where we harnessed, and I buried her there with her collar still on and the little metal tag that had the number 32, her number (and mine) in the Iditarod, and after a long time I went back to the house and sipped tea and thought of when she was young and there was nothing in front of us but the iceblink on the horizon, and I hoped wherever dogs go she would find a lot of good meat and fat and now and then a run.

DOG HEAVEN

Stephanie Vaughn

EVERY SO OFTEN THAT dead dog dreams me up again.

It's twenty-five years later. I'm walking along Forty-second Street in Manhattan, the sounds of the city crashing beside me — horns and gearshifts, insults — somebody's chewing gum holding my foot to the pavement, when that dog wakes from his long sleep and imagines me.

I'm sweet again. I'm sweet-breathed and flat-limbed. Our family is stationed at Fort Niagara, and the dog swims his red heavy fur into the black Niagara River. Across the street from the officers' quarters, down the steep shady bank, the river, even this far downstream, has been clocked at nine miles per hour. The dog swims after a stick I have thrown.

"Are you crazy?" my grandmother says, even though she is not fond of dog hair in the house, the way it sneaks into the refrigerator every time you open the door. "There's a current out there! It'll take that dog all the way to Toronto!"

"The dog knows where the backwater ends and the current begins," I say, because it is true. He comes down to the river all the time with my father, my brother MacArthur, or me. You never have to yell the dog away from the place where the river water moves like a whip.

Sparky Smith and I had a game we played called Knockout. It involved a certain way of breathing and standing up fast that caused the blood to leave the brain as if a plug had been jerked from the skull. You came to again just as soon as you were on the ground, the blood sloshing back, but it always seemed as if you had left the planet, had a vacation on Mars, and maybe stopped back at Fort Niagara half a lifetime later.

There weren't many kids my age on the post, because it was a small command. Most of its real work went on at the missile batteries flung like shale along the American-Canadian border. Sparky Smith and I hadn't been at Lewiston-Porter Central School long enough to get to know many people, so we entertained ourselves by meeting in a hollow of trees and shrubs at the far edge of the parade ground and telling each other seventh-grade sex jokes that usually had to do with keyholes and doorknobs, hot dogs and hot-dog buns, nuns, priests, preachers, schoolteachers, and people in blindfolds.

When we ran out of sex jokes, we went to Knockout and took turns catching each other as we fell like a cut tree toward the ground. Whenever I knocked out, I came to on the grass with the dog barking, yelping, crouching, crying for help. "Wake up! Wake up!" he seemed to say. "Do you know your name? Do you know your name? My name is Duke! My name is Duke!" I'd wake to the sky with the urgent call of the dog in the air, and I'd think, Well, here I am, back in my life again.

Sparky Smith and I spent our school time smiling too much and running for office. We wore mittens instead of gloves, because everyone else did. We made our mothers buy us ugly knit caps with balls on top — caps that in our previous schools would have identified us as weird but were part of the winter uniform in upstate New York. We wobbled onto the ice of the post rink, practicing in secret, banged our knees, scraped the palms of our hands, so that we would be invited to skating parties by civilian children.

"You skate?" With each other we practiced the cool look.

"Oh, yeah. I mean like I do it some — I'm not a racer or anything."

Every school morning, we boarded the Army-green bus — the slime-green, dead-swamp-algae-green bus — and rode it to the post gate, past the concrete island where the MPs stood in their bulletproof booth. Across from the gate, we got off at a street corner and waited with the other Army kids, the junior-high and high-school kids, for the real bus, the yellow one with the civilian kids on it. Just as we began to board, the civilian kids — there were only six of them but eighteen of us — would begin to sing the Artillery Song with obscene variations one of them had invented. Instead of "Over hill, over dale," they sang things like "Over boob, over tit." For a few weeks, we sat in silence watching the heavy oak trees of the town give way to apple orchards and potato farms, and we pretended not to hear. Then one day Sparky Smith began to sing the real Artillery Song, the booming song with caissons rolling along in it, and we all joined in and took over the bus with our voices.

When we ran out of verses, one of the civilian kids, a football player in high school, yelled, "Sparky is a *dog's* name. Here, Sparky, Sparky, Sparky." Sparky rose from his seat with

a wounded look, then dropped to the aisle on his hands and knees and bit the football player in the calf. We all laughed, even the football player, and Sparky returned to his seat.

"That guy's just lucky I didn't pee on his leg." Sparky said.

Somehow Sparky got himself elected homeroom president and me homeroom vice-president in January. He liked to say, "In actual percentages — I mean in actual per capita terms — we are doing much better than the civilian kids." He kept track of how many athletes we had, how many band members, who among the older girls might become a cheerleader. Listening to him even then, I couldn't figure out how he got anyone to vote for us. When he was campaigning, he sounded dull and serious, and anyway he had a large head and looked funny in his knit cap. He put up a homemade sign in the lunchroom, went from table to table to find students from 7-B to shake hands with, and said to me repeatedly, as I walked along a step behind him and nodded, "Just don't tell them that you're leaving in March. Under no circumstances let them know that you will not be able to finish out your term."

In January, therefore, I was elected homeroom vice-president by people I still didn't know (nobody in 7-B rode our bus — that gave us an edge), and in March my family moved to Fort Sill. in Oklahoma. I surrendered my vice-presidency to a civilian girl, and that was the end for all time of my career in public office.

Two days before we left Fort Niagara, we took the dog, Duke, to Charlie Battery, fourteen miles from the post, and left him with the mess sergeant. We were leaving him for only six weeks, until we could settle in Oklahoma and send for him. He had stayed at Charlie Battery before, when we visited our relatives in Ohio at Christmastime. He knew there were big meaty bones at Charlie Battery, and scraps of chicken, steak, turkey, slices of cheese, special big-dog bowls of ice cream. The mess at Charlie Battery was Dog Heaven, so he gave us a soft, forgiving look as we walked with him from the car to the back of the mess hall.

My mother said, as she always did at times like that, "I wish he knew more English." My father gave him a fierce manly scratch behind the ears. My brother and I scraped along behind with our pinched faces.

"Don't you worry," the sergeant said. "He'll be fine here. We like this dog, and he likes us. He'll run that fence perimeter all day long. He'll be his own early-warning defense system. Then we'll give this dog everything he ever dreamed of eating." The sergeant looked quickly at my father to see if the lighthearted reference to the defense system had been all right. My father was in command of the missile batteries. In my father's presence, no one spoke lightly of the defense of the United States of America — of the missiles that would rise from the earth like a wind and knock out (knock out!) the Soviet planes flying over the North Pole with their nuclear bombs. But Duke was my father's dog, too, and I think that my father had the same wish we all had — to tell him that we were going to send for him, this was just going to be a wonderful dog vacation.

"Sergeant Carter has the best mess within five hundred miles," my father said to me and MacArthur.

We looked around. We had been there for Thanksgiving dinner when the grass was still green. Now, in late winter, it was a dreary place, a collection of rain-streaked metal buildings standing near huge dark mounds of earth. In summer, the mounds looked something like the large grassy mounds in southern Ohio, the famous Indian mounds, softly rounded and benignly mysterious. In March, they were black with old snow. Inside the mounds were the Nike missiles, I supposed, although I didn't know for sure where the missiles were. Perhaps they were hidden in the depressions behind the mounds.

Once during "Fact Monday" in Homeroom 7-B, our teacher, Miss Bintz, had given a lecture on nuclear weapons. First she put a slide on the wall depicting an atom and its spinning electrons.

"Do you know what this is?" she said, and everyone in the room said, "An atom," in one voice, as if we were reciting a poem. We liked "Fact Monday" sessions because we didn't have to do any work for them. We sat happily in the dim light of her slides through lectures called "Nine Chapters in the Life of a Cheese" ("First the milk is warmed, then it is soured with rennet"), "The Morning Star of English Poetry" ("As springtime suggests the beginning of new life, so Chaucer stands at the beginning of English poetry"), and "Who's Who Among the Butterflies" ("The Monarch — *Anosia plexipus* — is king"). Sparky liked to say that Miss Bintz was trying to make us into third-graders again, but I liked Miss Bintz. She had high cheekbones and a passionate voice. She believed, like the adults in my family, that a fact was something solid and useful, like a penknife you could put in your pocket in case of emergency.

That day's lecture was "What Happens to the Atom When It's Smashed." Miss Bintz put on the wall a black-and-white slide of four women who had been horribly disfigured by the atomic blast at Hiroshima. The room was half darkened for the slide show. When she surprised us with the four faces of the women, you could feel the darkness grow, the silence in the bellies of the students.

"And do you know what this is?" Miss Bintz said. No one spoke. What answer could she have wanted from us, anyway? She clicked the slide machine through ten more pictures — close-ups of blistered hands, scarred heads, flattened buildings, burned trees, maimed and naked children staggering toward the camera as if the camera were food, a house, a mother, a father, a friendly dog.

"Do you know what this is?" Miss Bintz said again. Our desks were arranged around the edge of the room, creating an arena in the center. Miss Bintz entered that space and began to move along the front of our desks, looking to see who would answer her incomprehensible question.

"Do you know?" She stopped in front of my desk.

"No," I said.

"Do you know?" She stopped next at Sparky's desk.

Sparky looked down and finally said, "It's something horrible."

"That's right," she said. "It's something very horrible. This is the effect of an atom smashing. This is the effect of nuclear power." She turned to gesture at the slide, but she had stepped in front of the projector, and the smear of children's faces fell across her back. "Now let's think about how nuclear power got from the laboratory to the people of Japan." She had begun to pace again. "Let's think about where all this devastation and wreckage actually comes from. You tell me," she said to a large, crouching boy named Donald Anderson. He was hunched over his desk, and his arms lay before him like tree limbs.

"I don't know," Donald Anderson said.

"Of course you do," Miss Bintz said. "Where did all of this come from?"

None of us had realized yet that Miss Bintz's message was political. I looked beyond Donald Anderson at the drawn window shades. Behind them were plate-glass windows, a view of stiff red-oak leaves, the smell of wood smoke in the air. Across the road from the school was an orchard, beyond that a pasture, another orchard, and then the town of Lewiston, standing on the Niagara River seven miles upstream from the long row of redbrick Colonial houses that were the officers' quarters at Fort Niagara. Duke was down by the river, probably, sniffing at the reedy edge, his head lifting when ducks flew low over the water. Once the dog had come back to our house with a live fish in his mouth, a carp. Nobody ever believed that story except those of us who saw it: me, my mother and father and brother, my grandmother.

Miss Bintz had clicked to a picture of a mushroom cloud and was now saying, "And where did the bomb come from?" We were all tired of "Fact Monday" by then. Miss Bintz walked back to where Sparky and I were sitting. "You military children," she said. "You know where the bomb comes from. Why don't you tell us?" she said to me.

Maybe because I was tired, or bored, or frightened — I don't know — I said to Miss Bintz, looking her in the eye, "The bomb comes from the mother bomb."

Everyone laughed. We laughed because we needed to laugh, and because Miss Bintz had all the answers and all the questions and she was pointing them at us like guns.

"Stand up," she said. She made me enter the arena in front of the desks, and then she clicked the machine back to the picture of the Japanese women. "Look at this picture and make a joke," she said. What came next was the lecture she had been aiming for all along. The bomb came from the United States of America. We in the United States were worried about whether another country might use the bomb, but in the whole history of the human species only one country had ever used the worst weapon ever invented. On she went, bombs and airplanes and bomb tests, and then she got to the missiles. They were right here, she said, not more than ten miles away. Didn't we all know that? "You know that, don't you?" she said to me. If the missile weren't hidden among our orchards, the planes from the Soviet Union would not have any reason to drop bombs on top of Lewiston-Porter Central Junior High School.

I had stopped listening by then and realized that the pencil I still held in my hand was drumming a song against my thigh. Over hill, over dale. I looked back at the wall again, where the mushroom cloud had reappeared, and my own silhouette stood wildly in the middle of it. I looked at Sparky and dropped the pencil on the floor, stooped down to get it, looked at Sparky once more, stood up, and knocked out.

Later, people told me that I didn't fall like lumber, I fell like something soft collapsing, a fan folding in on itself, a balloon rumpling to the floor. Sparky saw what I was up to and tried to get out from behind his desk to catch me, but it was Miss Bintz I fell against, and she went down, too. When I woke up, the lights were on, the mushroom cloud was a pale ghost against the wall, voices in the room sounded like insect wings, and I was back in my life again.

"I'm so sorry," Miss Bintz said. "I didn't know you were an epileptic."

At Charlie Battery, it was drizzling as my parents stood and talked with the sergeant, rain running in dark tiny ravines along the slopes of the mounds.

MacArthur and I had M&M's in our pockets, which we were allowed to give to the dog for his farewell. When we extended our hands, though, the dog lowered himself to the gravel and looked up at us from under his tender red eyebrows. He seemed to say that if he took the candy he knew we would go, but if he didn't perhaps we would stay here at the missile battery and eat scraps with him.

We rode back to the post in silence, through the gray apple orchards, through small upstate towns, the fog rising out of the rain like a wish. MacArthur and I sat against opposite doors in the backseat, thinking of the loneliness of the dog.

We entered the kitchen, where my grandmother had already begun to clean the refrigerator. She looked at us, at our grim children's faces — the dog had been sent away a day earlier than was really necessary — and she said, "Well, God knows you can't clean the dog hair out of the house with the dog still in it."

Whenever I think of an Army post, I think of a place the weather cannot touch for long. The precise rectangles of the parade grounds, the precisely pruned trees and shrubs, the living quarters, the administration buildings, the PX and commissary, the nondenominational church, the teen club, the snack bar, the movie house, the skeet-and-trap field, the swimming pools, the runway, warehouses, the Officers' Club, the NCO Club. Men marching, women marching, saluting, standing at attention, at ease. The bugle will trumpet reveille, mess call, assembly, retreat, taps through a hurricane, a tornado, flood, blizzard. Whenever I think of the clean, squared look of a military post, I think that if one were blown down today in a fierce wind, it would be standing again tomorrow in time for reveille.

The night before our last full day at Fort Niagara, an Arctic wind slipped across the lake and froze the rain where it fell, on streets, trees, power lines, rooftops. We awoke to a fabulation of ice, the sun shining like a weapon, light rocketing off every surface except the surfaces of the Army's clean streets and walks.

MacArthur and I stood on the dry, scraped walk in front of our house and watched a jeep pass by on the way to the gate. On the post, everything was operational, but in the civilian world beyond the gate, power lines were down, hanging like daggers in the sun, roads were glazed with ice, cars were in ditches, highways were impassable. No yellow school buses were going to be on the roads that morning.

"This means we miss our very last day in school," MacArthur said. "No good-byes for us."

We looked up at the high, bare branches of the hard maples, where drops of ice glimmered.

"I just want to shake your hand and say so long," Sparky said. He had come out of his house to stand with us. "I guess you know this means you'll miss the surprise party."

"There was going to be a party?" I said.

"Just cupcakes," Sparky said. "I sure wish you could stay the school year and keep your office."

"Oh, who cares!" I said, suddenly irritated with Sparky, although he was my best friend. "Jesus," I said, sounding to myself like an adult — like Miss Bintz, maybe, when she was off duty.

"Jesus," I said again. "What kind of office is home god-dam room vice-president in a crummy country school?"

MacArthur said to Sparky, "What kind of cupcakes were they having?"

I looked down at MacArthur and said, "Do you know how totally ridiculous you look in that knit cap? I can't wait until we get out of this place."

"Excuse me," MacArthur said. "Excuse me for wearing the hat you gave me for my birthday."

It was then that the dog came back. We heard him calling out before we saw him, his huge woof-woof "My name is Duke! My name is Duke! I'm your dog! I'm your dog!" Then we saw him streaking through the trees, through the park space of oaks and maples between our house and the post gate. Later the MPs would say that he stopped and wagged his tail at them before he passed through the gate, as if he understood that he should be stopping to show his ID card. He ran to us, bounding across the crusted, glass-slick snow — ran into the history of our family, all the stories we would tell about him after he was dead. Years and years later, whenever we came back together at the family table, we would start the dog stories. He was the dog who caught the live fish with his mouth, the one who stole a pound of butter off the commissary loading dock and brought it to us in his soft bird dog's mouth without a tooth mark on the package. He was the dog who broke out of Charlie Battery the morning of an ice storm, traveled fourteen miles across the needled grasses of frozen pastures, through the prickly frozen mud of orchards, across backyard fences in small towns, and found the lost family.

The day was good again. When we looked back at the ice we saw a fairyland. The redbrick houses looked like ice castles. The ice-coated trees, with their million dreams of light, seemed to cast a spell over us.

"This is for you," Sparky said, and handed me a gold-foiled box. Inside were chocolate candies and a note that said, "I have enjoyed knowing you this year. I hope you have a good life." Then it said, "P.S. Remember this name. Someday I'm probably going to be famous."

"Famous as what?" MacArthur said.

"I haven't decided yet," Sparky said.

We had a party. We sat on the front steps of our quarters, Sparky, MacArthur, the dog, and I, and we ate all the chocolates at eight o'clock in the morning. We sat shoulder to shoulder, the four of us, and looked across the street through the trees at the river, and we talked about what we might be doing a year from then. Finally, we finished the chocolates and stopped talking and allowed the brilliant light of that morning to enter us.

Miss Bintz is the one who sent me the news about Sparky four months later. BOY DROWNS IN SWIFT CURRENT. In the newspaper story, Sparky takes the bus to Niagara Falls with two friends from Lewiston-Porter. It's a searing July day, a hundred degrees in the city, so the boys climb down the gorge into the river and swim in a place where it's illegal to swim, two miles downstream from the Falls. The boys Sparky is visiting — they're both student-council members as well as football players, just the kind of boys Sparky himself wants to be — have sneaked down to this swimming place many times: a cove in the bank of the river, where the water is still and glassy on a hot July day, not like the water raging in the middle of the river. But the current is a wild invisible thing, unreliable, whipping out with a looping arm to pull you in. "He was only three feet in front of me," one of the boys said. "He took one more stroke and then he was gone."

We were living in civilian housing not far from the post. When we had the windows open, we could hear the bugle calls and the sound of the cannon firing retreat at sunset. A month after I got the newspaper clipping about Sparky, the dog died. He was killed, along with every other dog on our block, when a stranger drove down our street one evening and threw poisoned hamburger into our front yards.

All that week I had trouble getting to sleep at night. One night I was still awake when the recorded bugle sounded taps, the sound drifting across the Army fences and into our bedrooms. Day is done, gone the sun. It was the sound of my childhood in sleep. The bugler played it beautifully, mournfully, holding fast to the long, high notes. That night I listened to the cadence of it, to the yearning of it. I thought of the dog again, only this time I suddenly saw him rising like a missile into the air, the red glory of his fur flying, his nose pointed heavenward. I remembered the dog leaping high, prancing on his hind legs the day he came back from Charlie

Battery, the dog rocking back and forth, from front legs to hind legs, dancing, sliding across the ice of the post rink later that day, as Sparky, MacArthur, and I played crack-the-whip, holding tight to each other, our skates careening and singing. "You're AWOL! You're AWOL!" we cried at the dog. "No school!" the dog barked back. "No school!" We skated across the darkening ice into the sunset, skated faster and faster, until we seemed to rise together into the cold, bright air. It was a good day, it was a good day, it was a good day.

THE DOG

Susan Schaeffer

There is everything in his eyes.
Everything.
Packs of wolves fleeing across the frozen waves,
Black shapes into the blacker woods
And he is there.
Once he was one of them

Such muscles in his legs,
Such thighs,
Such hinged jaws. A giant of a dog
Who barks at horses, sheep,
Mistaking them for the wolf he still is.

Today he lies on the rug,
Tail bandaged, a giant, a walking house
Brought down by fleas
And yet there are meadows in his eyes,
Steep, sharp cliffs toward which the sheep
Drift like suicidal clouds,
And as he dreams,
His muscles twitch,
In nightmares it is always the same,
He sees the danger, cannot raise his head,
Cannot bark or move.

When he opens his eyes,
He takes it all in, what has become of him,
His people, whom he loves,
Moving through such familiar rooms,
The small cat who dances by,
These things are his to keep.

Is he diminished?
He thinks not.
He says, I have known love
They touch my fur with love.
I have not sold my soul
For a safe haven, a handful of bones.

And yet, in dreams,
He is running free
And his people stream behind him
Like flags, like wind-tossed rags
Who will catch up with him
When he gets where he is going,
When he once more
Knows what he has always known.

DOG'S DEATH

John Updike

She must have been kicked unseen or brushed by a car.
Too young to know much, she was beginning to learn
To use the newspapers spread on the kitchen floor
And to win, wetting there, the words, "Good dog!
                                                                    Good dog!"

We thought her shy malaise was a shot reaction.
The autopsy disclosed a rupture in her liver.
As we teased her with play, blood was filling her skin
And her heart was learning to lie down forever.

Monday morning, as the children, were noisily fed
And sent to school, she crawled beneath the youngest's bed.
We found her twisted and limp but still alive.
In the car to the vet's, on my lap, she tried

To bite my hand and died. I stroked her warm fur
And my wife called in a voice imperious with tears.
Though surrounded by love that would have upheld her.
Nevertheless she sank and, stiffening, disappeared.

Back home, we found that in the night her frame,
Drawing near to dissolution, had endured the shame
Of diarrhoea and had dragged across the floor
To a newspaper carelessly left there. *Good dog.*

THE LOST DOG

Gene Hill

EVERY TIME I STOPPED, the moonlight seemed to carry the slight tinkle of the dog bell I was listening for so intently. I stood there, heron-like, one foot in the air, afraid to put it down for fear that the slightest noise might mute the one sound I was waiting for. But the evening was a mocking one — I felt I might well have been searching for a leprechaun or stalking the pot of gold at the end of a rainbow.

I had last seen Pat at about 10 A.M. when she had found and pointed a woodcock. When I shot, she broke, as usual, since I wasn't too meticulous on that nicety, and up in front of us flushed a prime whitetail buck. Before this Pat had been at worst a five-minute deer chaser, just a little run to satisfy her instincts. I hadn't been overly concerned, but this time as they flashed through the woods I had the feeling that five minutes wouldn't get the job done. Twelve hours later, as worried as I was angry, proved my hunch.

As English Setters go, Pat wasn't your "once–in–a–life-time dog." She was stubborn, willful, and vain. But I had trained her to the point where, when all went well, I could get a decent day's shooting over her. But when all didn't go well it could be a disaster. Many days I simply gave up and led her back to the kennel in the station wagon deciding to do the best I could by myself. I guess I kept her out for a variety of self-indulgent reasons: my refusal to admit I hadn't done as good a job of training as I should have; my tendency to spoil her and overlook the little hardheaded acts that usually led to bigger transgressions: and my plain soft-heartedness in refusing to come down harder and more often — a practice which might or might not have made a difference.

But by 10 P.M. all I could think of was a hurt dog lying in a roadside ditch waiting for me to find her, or a dog in the bottom of an abandoned well listening to my call and whistle and her answering bark tumbling back down on her in hollow, miserable mockery. I envisioned her collar hung on a wire fence, her foot in a forgotten fox trap. Anger and self-pity slowly gave way to fear and frustration so strong it nearly made me sick to my stomach. It was I who was the guilty one now and she the one needing desperately to have me with her.

I sat there listening to the night sounds... jet planes I'd rather have had been north winds. I'd rather the horns and screeching tires to have been the night calling of geese and herons. The sense of loss grew. Nothing comforted me. Everything seemed wrong. I felt like a small and simple man looking and listening for a lost dog while an impersonal, mechanical world went right on by without stopping to help or pausing to care.

The next day I told a friend I was upset about losing my dog, but he paid no attention to my grief; dogs are not worldly goods. That night I returned to where I had left my hunting coat with the slight belief that Pat would be there waiting for me. But the coat was an empty mockery of hope. I whistled and listened through yet another night, not knowing what else to do. Anxiety and fear were shoved aside by a feeling of futility and helplessness. The airplanes and traffic sounds made me feel more alone than ever before. I was on some strange sort of island.

I called the police but they showed little interest in only a lost dog. A check of neighboring houses and farms led to nothing. They promised to call if they saw a white English Setter but somehow I didn't feel encouraged. To them I was just an annoying stranger with a petty problem. I was a suspicious character to several, disbelieved by others, and, in my mind, ignored by all.

By now the night vigil had taken on another emotional aspect for I was searching for an unknown thing. Pat had become a symbol as real as any physical being. I needed to find her not only because I was committed to ending the mystery, but because I wanted to take her to these uncaring people and say, in effect, "Here is the dog I asked you about. See how much we enjoy each other; do you understand now how much it meant for me to have your help and understanding?" I wanted them to learn something about strangers and lost dogs and kindness, and caring enough to listen to the hurt of others with sympathy.

There was little sense in wandering around since Pat, no doubt, was doing the same thing, so I decided instead to find a spot to use as a post. I chose a long, slanting, fallen oak whose brandies had caught in another tree. I climbed up, rested my back against a limb, and watched the evening mist beneath me like a silken sea. Here, suspended in space and time, my imagination was free to create a scene of a dog running a deer for a day, then, just as she is about to give up and come home another deer jumps in front of her, and then another. Unable to stop herself, Pat is lead into a land she can never leave. I imagined a dog barking and another answering, then a third calling. My imagination flowed freely once again. One dog started barking and then dogs all across the country answered one another in an endless chain of howls in recognition of all that dogs have suffered at the hands of man in the cold light of the moon. I listened for a dog calling my name.

I placed a small ad in the local paper: LOST DOG, my name and telephone number, a description of Pat and the promise of a reward, but I had no faith in it. Almost a week had passed and I was running out of things to do; yet I felt I had to do something. The fading moon was just a twist of yellow like a discarded rind of lemon, making the night seem ominous. I brought a star book, laid back on my oak bed, and tried to memorize the Pleiades, Orion, and Betelgeuse. I thought of the ancient desert shepherds and their nighttime philosophies on the star. I thought of their naked minds relating the unrelatable, glibly marrying suspicion, myth, and astrology, and trying to find a meaningful place for themselves while being surrounded by nothing except the incredible extension of their intellect. And I was bewildered when I thought how much of it had really worked out after all. But, in the lone run, philosophy is a comfort only to philosophers and I am not really one of those incredible abstract thinkers — just a small, cold man lost in the woods; being hunted, I hoped, by a hungry, homesick bird dog.

I tried the old hunters trick of imagining what I would do if I was a lost dog. Where would I go? What would be the limits of my endurance? But this was idle foolishness. Pat could literally be anywhere — around the next turn or in another world. The night vigil had lost its feeling of function and I took to driving around more and sitting less. A pointless use of time perhaps, but maybe, just maybe, I would find Pat.

I gave up when over a week had passed. I took the kennel out of the station wagon and avoided going near the dog run by the barn. My family had long since stopped talking about hunting in an effort to be kind to me, but it didn't matter. My own feelings were mixed: a sense of loss, a deep guilt, and worst of all, a nagging uncertainty. I didn't really believe Pat was gone. I couldn't conceive or cope with the idea of forever. I still drove around the area where she had run away, but more like a person trying to wake up from a bad dream than from any real hope of seeing her sitting by the side of the road listening for the familiar sound of my car. People would recognize my car and wave, and a couple of kids knew me as the "lost dog man."

My mind searched for a simple solution. I imagined Pat had been hit by a passing car, then crawled into the woods and gone to sleep, undetected by the driver. It was neat, logical, likely — and unsatisfactory. Other possibilities came to mind but none were any better.

After two weeks the painful sense of loss faded, leaving a numb feeling of emptiness. I still caught myself listening for her bark when I pulled in the driveway, but the empty spots where she used to lie seemed ordinary again and I didn't think about feeding time anymore. I felt better when I reminded myself that she was just an ordinary working field dog, nothing to brag about, spoiled, mischievous — and yet it hurt to remember that Pat was my dog in every sense of the word. She followed me everywhere, slept by my chair when I let her in the house and loved riding in the front seat of the car. The simple truth was that Pat had gotten to me in her own way, more than I had been readily willing to admit before. I felt almost ashamed to be so sentimental. It was difficult to imagine a man my age crying alone in his car for the sight of a small white dog. But it happened, and happened more than once.

This was all some time ago and I've never seen or heard of Pat again. I'm past grief now. Her image in my memory remains like a poorly focused snapshot of a white dog off in an alder thicket — indistinct and distant like a ghost or a drifting wraith of mist.

They say that time heals all wounds, but that's not wholly true. Sometimes we can work around the reality and believe in a hereafter when we have to — imagining a lost dog living with someone else far away — a kind and gentle master who has discovered that she loves to ride in the front seat of the car with the window open, hates peanut butter sandwiches, and will, for no apparent reason, cock her head and stand stock still for the long-est time as if she were listening for a faint whistling carried on the evening wind and the calling of a name she still remembers.

TO ABSENT FRIENDS

EULOGY

by Jameson Parker

I TOOK MY OLD FRIEND to the vet yesterday and had him put to sleep. The staff of the clinic must all have been alerted by my wife because the receptionist recognized my name or his on the sign-in sheet and said "Oh," with a significance that made my heart turn over and she showed me immediately into one of the little rooms. Examining rooms. Rooms of healing, rooms of death, which is sometimes, ultimately, the only possible healing left us. Almost instantly a new and unknown vet, improbably young, came in with an assistant. They asked me if I had ever been present at a euthanasia before. They asked me to have Max lie down.

"Sit, old man," I said, and in a final irony the failing hips, which were one of the primary reasons for this fatal trip, worked perfectly.

"Lie down," I said and he lay down as he had always lain, at my feet, panting slightly from nerves. He was always nervous at the vet's. I should have had them come out to the house.

The child vet took the prepared syringe she had brought in, felt quickly and expertly for the vein in Max's right leg and administered the shot. As the syringe emptied, he stopped panting and gently lowered his nose forward onto the ground just outside his leg, as he was wont to do, and slept for the last time.

Surely something as momentous as the dark magnitude of death must give us some kind of epiphany, reward us at least with a moment of transcendent understanding of life, of what it means to be not just a human but any living thing on this shared earth, provide us some insight into the relationship between man and his kindly mentor and willing servant. Surely it should give me words to express these acute insights and so ease my pain and make his quiet sleep worthwhile. But all that came out of my mouth as I stroked the thick, soft, still-warm ears — so much heavier than just a moment ago — was, "I'm sorry. I'm sorry. I'm sorry. I'm so sorry."

Sorry that I had neither skill enough nor prayers strong enough to fix the degenerate hips, the uncertain bowels, to prolong, pain free and dignity intact, the life that had given me such pleasure. But when that pale and unrelenting trainer blows his silent whistle for us we must go, skill nor prayers notwithstanding.

What I wept for, selfishly, was not just a dog, though there is no such thing as "just a dog" anymore than there is "just a child" or "just a wife" or "just a father," but rather for an irretrievable part of my heart, for twelve years of my life that were immeasurably enriched by his presence, and ultimately for the godlike forgiveness of sins, oh so many sins, washed away by a rough pink tongue, absolved by the drumming of a loving tail. How ironic, how incredible, that in the relationship between man and dog we should be given the role of God, for we are so woefully miscast.

In the end what you're left with is doubt and pain. Doubt of your own judgement, your own motives. Was the discomfort of his deteriorating hips great enough to justify this? Was it an act of kindness or a selfish reaction to the inconvenience of incontinence? Could I have done more? Should I have tried something else? And pain — exquisite, excruciating pain. If life is a system of balances, of yin and yang, birth and death, light and dark, then the proof of the great pleasure he gave me lies in the quantity of pain his passing has caused. For twelve years he was my friend, my true and constant companion, my mentor, for God knows I learned more about hunting from him than he learned about retrieving from me.

Moments of triumph. The grouse he found where I knew there would be no grouse, could be no grouse because I had read the books and he hadn't. The impossible retrieve against insuperable life threatening odds in a fast flowing river where I had misjudged the current, a retrieve I should never have asked for. The pheasants found, bird after bird after bird, flushed and retrieved in a field previously picked clean by other hunters, other dogs, and him on already-weakening ten-year-old legs. And then as we walked back triumphant, exultant, limited out, we found an old cemetery hidden and overgrown on the edge of a slough and as we stopped to read the headstones, for the first time in his great-hearted life he sank slowly to the ground and could not go on. I thought then my heart would break. Other moments, equally memorable, if not so eminent. The high Sierra lake where I took my children, my handicapped daughter using his thick powerful tail as a tow rope while he churned happily through the water, hour on end like the lifeguard he was. The end of a long day's grouse hunting as we dragged our weary bodies back to my brand new station wagon and Max decided, for the only time in his life, to roll in a dead animal, but made up for all other abstinences by choosing to roll in a dead skunk. We walked the seven miles home.

And a thousand other memories common to all hunters and all who love dogs, nothing unique, nothing extraordinary. And yet... And yet there will always be galloping toward me a joyous brown dog with eyes the color of a good single malt whiskey, goose, pheasant or quail in his mouth, bringing the bird to me, giving me always far more than I could ever have give him.

WINTER DOG

Alistair Macleod

I AM WRITING THIS in December. In the period close to
Christmas, and three days after the first snowfall in this
region of southwestern Ontario. The snow came quietly in
the night or in the early morning. When we went to bed
near midnight, there was none at all. Then early in the
morning we heard the children singing Christmas songs
from their rooms across the hall. It was very dark and I
rolled over to check the time. It was four-thirty A.M. One of
them must have awakened and looked out the window to
find the snow and then eagerly awakened the others. They
are half crazed by the promise of Christmas, and the discov-
ery of the snow is an unexpected giddy surprise. There was
no snow promised for this area, not even yesterday.

"What are you doing?" I call, although it is obvious.

"Singing Christmas songs," they shout back with equal
obviousness, "because it snowed."

"Try to be quiet," I say, "or you'll wake the baby."

"She's already awake," they say. "She's listening to our singing. She likes it. Can we go out and make a snowman?"

I roll from my bed and go to the window. The neighboring houses are muffled in snow and silence and there are as yet no lights in any of them. The snow has stopped falling and its whitened quietness reflects the shadows of the night.

"This snow is no good for snowmen," I say. "It is too dry."

"How can snow be dry?" asks a young voice. Then an older one says, "Well, then can we go out and make the first tracks?"

They take my silence for consent and there are great sounds of rustling and giggling as they go downstairs to touch the light switches and rummage and jostle for coats and boots.

"What on earth is happening?" asks my wife from her bed. "What are they doing?"

"They are going outside to make the first tracks in the snow," I say. "It snowed quite heavily last night."

"What time is it?"

"Shortly after four-thirty."

"Oh."

We ourselves have been nervous and restless for the past weeks. We have been troubled by illness and uncertainty in those we love far away on Canada's east coast. We have already considered and rejected driving the fifteen hundred miles. Too far, too uncertain, too expensive, fickle weather, the complications of transporting Santa Claus.

Instead, we sleep uncertainly and toss in unbidden

dreams. We jump when the phone rings after ten P.M. and are then reassured by the distant voices.

"First of all, there is nothing wrong," they say. "Things are just the same."

Sometimes we make calls ourselves, even to the hospital in Halifax, and are surprised at the voices which answer.

"I just got here this afternoon from Newfoundland. I'm going to try to stay a week. He seems better today. He's sleeping now."

At other times we receive calls from farther west, from Edmonton and Calgary and Vancouver. People hoping to find objectivity in the most subjective of situations. Strung out in uncertainty across the time zones from British Columbia to Newfoundland.

Within our present city, people move and consider possibilities:

If he dies tonight we'll leave right away. Can you come?

We will have to drive as we'll never get air reservations at this time.

I'm not sure if my car is good enough. I'm always afraid of the mountains near Cabano.

If we were stranded in Riviere du Loup we would be worse off than being here. It would be too far for anyone to come and get us.

My car will go but I'm not so sure I can drive it all the way. My eyes are not so good anymore, especially at night in drifting snow.

Perhaps there'll be no drifting snow.

There's always drifting snow.

We'll take my car if you'll drive it. We'll have to drive straight through.

John phoned and said he'll give us his car if we want it or he'll drive — either his own car or someone else's.

He drinks too heavily, especially for long-distance driving, and at this time of year. He's been drinking ever since this news began.

He drinks because he cares. It's just the way he is.

Not everybody drinks.

Not everybody cares, and if he gives you his word, he'll never drink until he gets there. We all know that.

But so far nothing has happened. Things seem to remain the same.

Through the window and out on the white plane of the snow, the silent, laughing children now appear. They move in their muffled clothes like mummers on the whitest of stages. They dance and gesture noiselessly, flopping their arms in parodies of heavy, happy, earthbound birds. They have been warned by the eldest to be aware of the sleeping neighbors so they cavort only in pantomime, sometimes raising mittened hands to their mouths to suppress their joyous laughter. They dance and prance in the moonlight, tossing snow in one another's direction, tracing out various shapes and initials forming lines which snake across the previously unmarked whiteness. All of it in silence, unknown and unseen and unheard to the neighboring world. They seem unreal even to me, their father, standing at his darkened window. It is almost as if they have danced out of the world of folklore like happy elves who cavort and mimic and caper through the private hours of this whitened dark, only to vanish with the coming of the morning's light and leaving only the signs of their activities behind. I am tempted to check the recently vacated beds to confirm what perhaps I think I know.

Then out of the corner of my eye I see him. The golden collie-like dog. He appears almost as if from the wings of the stage or as a figure newly noticed in the lower corner of a winter painting. He sits quietly and watches the playful scene before him and then, as if responding to a silent invitation, bounds into its midst. The children chase him in frantic circles, falling and rolling as he doubles back and darts and dodges between their legs and through their outstretched arms. He seizes a mitt loosened from its owner's hand, and tosses it happily in the air and then snatches it back into his jaws an instant before it reaches the ground and seconds before the tumbling bodies fall on the emptiness of its expected destination. He races to the edge of the scene and lies facing them, holding the mitt tantalizingly between his paws, and then as they dash towards him, he leaps forward again, tossing and catching it before him and zigzagging through them as the Sunday football player might return the much sought-after ball. After he has gone through and eluded them all, he looks back over his shoulder and again, like an elated athlete, tosses the mitt high in what seems like an imaginary end zone. Then he seizes it once more and lopes in a wide circle around his pursuers, eventually coming closer and closer to them until once more their stretching hands are able to actually touch his shoulders and back and haunches, although he continues always to wriggle free. He is touched but never captured, which is the nature of the game. Then he is gone. As suddenly as he came. I strain my eyes in the direction of the adjoining street, towards the house where I have often seen him, always within a yard enclosed by woven links of chain. I see the flash of his silhouette, outlined perhaps against the snow or the light cast by the street lamps or the moon. It arcs upwards and seems to hang for an instant high above the top of the fence and then it descends on the other side. He lands on his shoulder in a fluff of snow and with a half roll regains his feet and vanishes within the shadow of his owner's house.

"What are you looking at?" asks my wife.

"That golden collie-like dog from the other street was just playing with the children in the snow."

"But he's always in that fenced-in yard."

"I guess not always. He jumped the fence just now and went back in. I guess the owners and the rest of us think he's fenced in but he knows he's not. He probably comes out every night and leads an exciting life. I hope they don't see his tracks or they'll probably begin to chain him."

"What are the children doing?"

"They look tired now from chasing the dog. They'll probably soon be back in. I think I'll go downstairs and wait for them and make myself a cup of coffee."

"Okay."

I look once more towards the fenced-in yard but the dog is nowhere to be seen.

I first saw such a dog when I was twelve and he came

as a pup of about two months in a crate to the railroad station which was about eight miles from where we lived. Someone must have phoned or dropped in to say: "Your dog's at the station."

He had come to Cape Breton in response to a letter and a check which my father had sent to Mornsburg, Ontario. We had seen the ads for "cattle collie dogs" in the *Family Herald*, which was the farm newspaper of the time, and we were in need of a good young working dog.

His crate was clean and neat and there was still a supply of dog biscuits with him and a can in the corner to hold water. The baggage handlers had looked after him well on the trip east, and he appeared in good spirits. He had a white collar and chest and four rather large white paws and a small white blaze on his forehead. The rest of him was a fluffy, golden brown, although his eyebrows and the tips of his ears as well as the end of his tail were darker, tingeing almost to black. When he grew to his full size the blackish shadings became really black, and although he had the long, heavy coat of a collie, it was in certain areas more gray than gold. He was also taller than the average collie and with a deeper chest. He seemed to be at least part German shepherd.

It was winter when he came and we kept him in the house where he slept behind the stove in a box lined with an old coat. Our other dogs slept mostly in the stables or out-side in the lees of woodpiles or under porches or curled up on the banking of the house. We seemed to care more for him because he was smaller and it was winter and he was somehow like a visitor, and also because more was expected of him and also perhaps because we had paid money for him and thought about his coming for some time — like a "planned" child. Skeptical neighbors and relatives who thought the idea of paying money for a dog was rather exotic or frivolous would ask: "Is that your Ontario dog?" or "Do you think your Ontario dog will be any good?"

He turned out to be no good at all and no one knew why. Perhaps it was because of the suspected German shepherd blood. But he could not "get the hang of it." Although we worked him and trained him as we had other dogs, he seemed always to bring panic instead of order and to make things worse instead of better. He became a "head dog," which meant that instead of working behind the cattle he lunged at their heads, impeding them from any forward motion and causing them to turn in endless, meaningless bewildered circles. On the few occasions when he did go behind them, he was rough which meant that instead of being a floating, nipping, suggestive presence, he actually bit them and caused them to gallop, which was another sin. Sometimes in the summer the milk cows suffering from his misunderstood pursuit would jam pell-mell into the stable, tossing their wide horns in fear and with their great sides heaving and perspiring while down their legs and tails the wasted milk ran in rivulets mingling with the blood caused by his slashing wounds. He was, it was said, "worse than nothing."

Gradually everyone despaired, although he continued to grow gray and golden and was, as everyone agreed, a "beautiful-looking dog."

He was also tremendously strong and in the winter
months I would hitch him to a sleigh which he pulled easily
and willingly on almost any kind ot surface. When he was
harnessed I used to put a collar around his neck and attach a
light line to it so that I might have some minimum control
over him, but it was hardly ever needed. He would pull
home the Christmas tree or the bag of flour or the deer
which was shot far back in the woods and when we visited
our winter snares he would pull home the gunnysacks which
contained the partridges and rabbits which we gathered. He
would also pull us, especially on the flat windswept stretches
of land beside the sea. There the snow was never really deep
and the water that oozed from a series of freshwater springs
and ponds contributed to a glaze of ice and crisply crusted
snow which the sleigh runners seemed to sing over without
ever breaking through. He would begin with an easy lope
and then increase his swiftness until both he and the sleigh
seemed to touch the surface at only irregular intervals. He
would stretch out then with his ears flattened against his
head and his shoulders bunching and contracting in the
rhythm of his speed. Behind him on the sleigh we would
cling tenaciously to the wooden slats as the particles of ice
and snow dislodged by his nails hurtled towards our faces.
We would avert our heads and close our eyes and the wind
stung so sharply that the difference between freezing and
burning could not be known. He would do that until late in
the afternoon when it was time to return home and begin
our chores.

On the sunny winter Sunday that I am thinking of, I

planned to visit my snares. There seemed no other children around that afternoon and the adults were expecting relatives. I harnessed the dog to the sleigh, opened the door of the house and shouted that I was going to look at my snares. We began to climb the hill behind the house on our way to the woods when we looked back and out towards the sea. The "big ice," which was what we called the major pack of drift ice, was in solidly against the shore and stretched out beyond the range of vision. It had not been "in" yesterday, although for the past weeks we had seen it moving offshore, sometimes close and sometimes distant, depending on the winds and tides. The coming of the big ice marked the official beginning of the coldest part of winter. It was mostly drift ice from the Arctic and Labrador, although some of it was freshwater ice from the estuary of the St Lawrence. It drifted down with the dropping temperatures, bringing its own mysterious coldness and stretching for hundreds of miles in craters and pans, sometimes in grotesque shapes and sometimes in dazzling architectural forms. It was blue and white and sometimes gray and at other times a dazzling emerald green.

The dog and I changed our direction towards the sea, to find what the ice might yield. Our land had always been beside the sea and we had always gone towards it to find newness and the extraordinary; and over the years we, as others along the coast, had found quite a lot, although never the pirate chests of gold which were supposed to abound or the reasons for the mysterious lights that our elders still spoke of and persisted in seeing. But kegs of rum had washed up, and sometimes bloated horses and various fishing paraphernalia and valuable timber and furniture from foundered ships. The door of my room was apparently the galley door from a ship called the *Judith Franklin*, which was wrecked during the early winter in which my great-grandfather was building his house. My grandfather told of how they had heard the cries and seen the lights as the ship neared the rocks and of how they had run down in the dark and tossed lines to the people while tying themselves to trees on the shore. All were saved, including women clinging to small children. The next day the builders of the new house went down to the shore and salvaged what they could from the wreckage of the vanquished ship. A sort of symbolic marriage of the new and the old: doors and shelving, stairways, hatches, wooden chests and trunks and various glass figurines and lanterns which were miraculously never broken.

People came too. The dead as well as the living. Bodies of men swept overboard and reported lost at sea and the bodies of men still crouched within the shelter of their boats' broken bows. And sometimes in late winter young sealers who had quit their vessels would walk across the ice and come to our doors. They were usually very young — some still in their teens — and had signed on for jobs they could not or no longer wished to handle. They were often disoriented and did not know where they were, only that they had seen land and had decided to walk towards it. They were often frostbitten and with little money and uncertain as to how they might get to Halifax.

The dog and I walked towards the ice upon the sea.

Sometimes it was hard to "get on" the ice, which meant that at the point where the pack met the shore there might be open water or irregularities caused by the indentations of the coastline or the workings of the tides and currents, but for us on that day there was no difficulty at all. We were on easily and effortlessly and enthused in our new adventure. For the first mile there was nothing but the vastness of the white expanse. We came to a clear stretch where the ice was as smooth and unruffled as that of an indoor arena and I knelt on the sleigh while the dog loped easily along. Gradually the ice changed to an uneven terrain of pressure ridges and hummocks, making it impossible to ride farther; and then suddenly, upon rounding a hummock, I saw the perfect seal. At first I thought it was alive, as did the dog who stopped so suddenly in his tracks that the sleigh almost collided with his legs. The hackles on the back of his neck rose and he growled in the dangerous way he was beginning to develop. But the seal was dead, yet facing us in a frozen perfection that was difficult to believe. There was a light powder of snow over its darker coat and a delicate rime of frost still formed the outline of its whiskers. Its eyes were wide open and it stared straight ahead towards the land. Even now in memory it seems more real than reality — as if it were transformed by frozen art into something more arresting than life itself. The way the sudden seal in the museum exhibit freezes your eyes with the touch of truth. Immediately I wanted to take it home.

It was frozen solidly in a base of ice so I began to look for something that might serve as a pry. I let the dog out of his harness and hung the sleigh and harness on top of the hummock to mark the place and began my search. Some distance away I found a pole about twelve feet long. It is always surprising to find such things on the ice field but they are, often amazingly, there, almost in the same way that you might find a pole floating in the summer ocean. Unpredictable but possible. I took the pole back and began my work. The dog went off on explorations of his own.

Although it was firmly frozen, the task did not seem impossible and by inserting the end of the pole under first one side and then the other and working from the front to the back, it was possible to cause a gradual loosening. I remember thinking how very warm it was because I was working hard and perspiring heavily. When the dog came back he was uneasy, and I realized it was starting to snow a bit but I was almost done. He sniffed with disinterest at the seal and began to whine a bit, which was something he did not often do. Finally, after another quarter of an hour, I was able to roll my trophy onto the sleigh and with the dog in harness we set off. We had gone perhaps two hundred yards when the seal slid free. I took the dog and the sleigh back and once again managed to roll the seal on. This time I took the line from the dog's collar and tied the seal to the sleigh, reasoning that the dog would go home anyway and there would be no need to guide him. My fingers were numb as I tried to fasten the awkward knots and the dog began to whine and rear. When I gave the command he bolted forward and I clung at the back of the sleigh to the seal. The snow was heavier now and blowing in my face but we were moving rapidly and when we came to the stretch of arena-like ice we skimmed across it almost like an iceboat, the profile of the frozen seal at the front of the sleigh like those figures at the prows of Viking ships. At the very end of the smooth stretch, we went through. From my position at the end ot the sleigh I felt him drop almost before I saw him, and rolled backwards seconds before the sleigh and seal followed him into the blackness of the water. He went under once carried by his own momentum but surfaced almost immediately with his head up and his paws scrambling at the icy, jagged edge of the hole; but when the weight and momentum of the sleigh and its burden struck he went down again, this time out of sight.

I realized we had struck a "seam" and that the stretch of smooth ice had been deceivingly and temporarily joined to the rougher ice near the shore and now was in the process of breaking away. I saw the widening line before me and jumped to the other side just as his head miraculously came up once more. I lay on my stomach and grabbed his collar in both my hands and then in a moment of panic did not know what to do. I could feel myself sliding towards him and the darkness of the water and was aware of the weight that pulled me forward and down. I was also aware of his razor-sharp claws flailing violently before my face and knew that I might lose my eyes. And I was aware that his own eyes were bulging from their sockets and that he might think I was trying to choke him and might lunge and slash my face with his teeth in desperation. I knew all of this but somehow did nothing about it; it seemed almost simpler to hang on and be drawn into the darkness of the gently slopping water,

To Absent Friends

seeming to slop gently in spite of all the agitation. Then suddenly he was free, scrambling over my shoulder and dragging the sleigh behind him. The seal surfaced again, buoyed up perhaps by the physics of its frozen body or the nature of its fur. Still looking more genuine than it could have in life, its snout and head broke the open water and it seemed to look at us curiously for an instant before it vanished permanently beneath the ice. The loose and badly tied knots had apparently not held when the sleigh was in a near-vertical position and we were saved by the ineptitude of my own numbed ringers. We had been spared for a future time.

He lay gasping and choking for a moment, coughing up the icy salt water, and then almost immediately his coat began to freeze. I realized then how cold I was myself and that even in the moments I had been lying on the ice, my clothes had begun to adhere to it. My earlier heated perspiration was now a cold rime upon my body and I imagined it outlining me there, beneath my clothes, in a sketch of frosty white. I got on the sleigh once more and crouched low as he began to race towards home. His coat was freezing fast, and as he ran the individual ice-coated hairs began to clack together like rhythmical castanets attuned to the motion of his body. It was snowing quite heavily in our faces now and it seemed to be approaching dusk, although I doubted if it were so on the land which I could now no longer see. I realized all the obvious things I should have considered earlier. That if the snow was blowing in our faces, the wind was off the land, and if it was off the land, it was blowing the ice pack back out to sea. That was probably one reason why the seam had opened. And also that the ice had only been in one night and had not had a chance to set. I realized other things as well. That it was the time of the late afternoon when the tide was falling. That no one knew where we were. That I had said we were going to look at snares, which was not where we had gone at all. And I remembered now that I had received no answer even to that misinformation, so perhaps I had not even been heard. And also if there was drifting snow like this on land, our tracks would by now have been obliterated.

We came to a rough section of ice: huge slabs on their sides and others piled one on top of the other as if they were in some strange form of storage. It was no longer possible to ride the sleigh but as I stood up I lifted it and hung on to it as a means of holding on to the dog. The line usually attached to his collar had sunk with the vanished seal. My knees were stiff when I stood up; and deprived of the wind-break effect which the dog had provided, I felt the snow driving full into my face, particularly my eyes. It did not merely impede my vision, the way distant snow flurries might, but actually entered my eyes, causing them to water and freeze nearly shut. I was aware of the weight of ice on my eyelashes and could see them as they gradually lowered and became heavier. I did not remember ice like this when I got on, although I did not find that terribly surprising. I pressed the soles of my numbed feet firmly down upon it to try to feel if it was moving out, but it was impossible to tell because there was no fixed point of reference. Almost the sensation one gets on a conveyor belt at airports or on escalators; although you are standing still you recognize motion, but should you shut your eyes and be deprived of sight, even that recognition may become ambiguously uncertain.

The dog began to whine and to walk around me in circles, binding my legs with the traces of the harness as I continued to grasp the sleigh. Finally I decided to let him go as there seemed no way to hold him and there was nothing else to do. I unhitched the traces and doubled them up as best I could and tucked them under the backpad of his harness so they would not drag behind him and become snagged on any obstacles. I did not take off my mitts to do so as I was afraid I would not be able to get them back on. He vanished into the snow almost immediately.

The sleigh had been a gift from an uncle, so I hung on to it and carried it with both hands before me like an ineffectual shield against the wind and snow. I lowered my head as much as I could and turned it sideways so the wind would beat against my head instead of directly into my face.

Sometimes I would turn and walk backwards for a few steps. Although I knew it was not the wisest thing to do, it seemed at times the only way to breathe. And then I began to feel the water sloshing about my feet. Sometimes when the tides or currents ran heavily and the ice began to separate, the water that was beneath it would well up and wash over it almost as if it were reflooding it. Sometimes you could see the hard ice clearly beneath the water but at other times a sort of floating slush was formed mingling with snow and "slob" ice which was not yet solid. It was thick and dense and soupy and it was impossible to see what lay beneath it. Experienced men on the ice sometimes carried a slender pole so they could test the consistency of the footing which might or might not lie before them, but I was obviously not one of them, although I had a momentary twinge for the pole I had used to dislodge the seal. Still, there was nothing to do but go forward.

When I went through, the first sensation was almost of relief and relaxation for the water initially made me feel much warmer than I had been on the surface. It was the most dangerous of false sensations for I knew my clothes were becoming heavier by the second. I clung to the sleigh somewhat as a raft and lunged forward with it in a kind of up-and-down swimming motion, hoping that it might strike some sort of solidity before my arms became so weighted and sodden that I could no longer lift them. I cried out then for the first time into the driving snow.

He came almost immediately, although I could see he was afraid and the slobbing slush was up to his knees. Still, he seemed to be on some kind of solid footing for he was not swimming. I splashed towards him and when almost there, desperately threw the sleigh before me and lunged for the edge of what seemed like his footing, but it only gave way as if my hands were closing on icy insubstantial porridge. He moved forward then, although I still could not tell if what supported him would be of any use to me. Finally I grasped the breast strap of his harness. He began to back up then, and as I said, he was tremendously strong. The harness began to slide forward on his shoulders but he continued to pull as I continued to grasp and then I could feel my elbows on what seemed like solid ice and I was able to hook them on the edge and draw myself, dripping and soaking, like another seal out of the black water and onto the whiteness of the slushy ice. Almost at once my clothes began to freeze. My elbows and knees began to creak when I bent them as if I were a robot from the realm of science fiction and then I could see myself clothed in transparent ice as if I had been coated with shellac or finished with clear varnish.

As the fall into the winter sea had at first seemed ironically warm, so now my garments of ice seemed a protection against the biting wind, but I knew it was a deceptive sensation and that I did not have much time before me. The dog faced into the wind and I followed him. This time he stayed in sight, and at times even turned back to wait for me. He was cautious but certain and gradually the slush disappeared, and although we were still in water, the ice was hard and clear beneath it. The frozen heaviness of my clothes began to weigh on me and I could feel myself, ironically, perspiring within my suit of icy armor. I was very tired, which I knew was another dangerous sensation. And then I saw the land. It was very close and a sudden surprise. Almost like coming upon a stalled and unexpected automobile in a highway's winter storm. It was only yards away, and although there was no longer any ice actually touching the shore, there were several pans of it floating in the region between. The dog jumped from one to the other and I followed him, still clutching the sleigh, and missing only the last pan which floated close to the rocky shore. The water came only to my waist and I was able to touch the bottom and splash noisily on land. We had been spared again for a future time and I was never to know whether he had reached the shore himself and come back or whether he had heard my call against the wind.

We began to run towards home and the land lightened and there were touches of evening sun. The wind still blew but no snow was falling. Yet when I looked back, the ice and the ocean were invisible in the swirling squalls. It was like looking at another far and distant country on the screen of a snowy television.

I became obsessed, now that I could afford the luxury, with not being found disobedient or considered a fool. The visitors' vehicles were still in the yard so I imagined most of the family to be in the parlor or living room, and I circled the house and entered through the kitchen, taking the dog with me. I was able to get upstairs unnoticed and get my clothes changed and when I came down I mingled with everybody and tried to appear as normal as I could. My own family was caught up with the visitors and only general comments came my way. The dog, who could not change his clothes, lay under the table with his head on his paws and he was also largely unnoticed. Later as the ice melted from his coat, a puddle formed around him, which I casually mopped up. Still later someone said, "I wonder where that dog has been, his coat is soaking wet." I was never to tell anyone of the afternoon's experience or that he had saved my life.

Two winters later I was sitting at a neighbor's kitchen table when I looked out the window and saw the dog as he was shot. He had followed my father and also me and had been sitting rather regally on a little hill beside the house and I suppose had presented an ideal target. But he had moved at just the right or wrong time and instead of killing him the high-powered bullet smashed into his shoulder. He jumped into the air and turned his snapping teeth upon the wound, trying to bite the cause of the pain he could not see. And then he turned towards home, unsteady but still strong on his three remaining legs. No doubt he felt, as we all do, that if he could get home he might be saved, but he did not make it, as we knew he could not, because of the amount of blood on the snow and the wavering pattern of his three-legged tracks. Yet he was, as I said, tremendously strong and he managed almost three quarters of a mile. The house he sought must have been within his vision when he died for we could see it quite clearly when we came to his body by the roadside. His eyes were open and his tongue was clenched between his teeth and the little blood he had left dropped red and black on the winter snow. He was not to be saved for a future time anymore.

I learned later that my father had asked the neighbor to shoot him and that we had led him into a kind of ambush. Perhaps my father did so because the neighbor was younger and had a better gun or was a better shot. Perhaps because my father did not want to be involved. It was obvious he had not planned on things turning out so messy.

The dog had become increasingly powerful and protective, to the extent that people were afraid to come into the yard. And he had also bitten two of the neighbor's children and caused them to be frightened of passing our house on their journeys to and from school. And perhaps there was also the feeling in the community that he was getting more than his share of the breeding: that he traveled farther than other dogs on his nightly forays and that he fought off and injured the other smaller dogs who might compete with him for female favors. Perhaps there was fear that his dominance and undesirable characteristics did not bode well for future generations.

This has been the writing down of a memory triggered by the sight of a golden dog at play in the silent snow with my own excited children. After they came in and had their hot chocolate, the wind began to blow; and by the time I left for work, there was no evidence of their early-morning revels or any dog tracks leading to the chain-link fence. The "enclosed" dog looked impassively at me as I brushed the snow from the buried windshield. What does he know? he seemed to say.

The snow continues to drift and to persist as another uncertainty added to those we already have. Should we be forced to drive tonight, it will be a long, tough journey into the wind and the driving snow which is pounding across Ontario and Quebec and New Brunswick and against the granite coast of Nova Scotia. Should we be drawn by death, we might well meet our own. Still, it is only because I am alive that I can even consider such possibilities. Had I not been saved by the golden dog, I would not have these tight concerns or children playing in the snow or of course these memories. It is because of him that I have been able to come this far in time.

It is too bad that I could not have saved him as well and my feelings did him little good as I looked upon his bloodied body there beside the road. It was too late and out of my control and even if I had known the possibilities of the future it would not have been easy.

He was with us only for a while and brought his own changes, and yet he still persists. He persists in my memory and in my life and he persists physically as well. He is there in this winter storm. There in the golden-gray dogs with their black-tipped ears and tails, sleeping in the stables or in the lees of woodpiles or under porches or curled beside the houses which face towards the sea.

THE PRAYER OF THE DOG

Carmen Bernos De Gasztold,
translated by Rumen Godden

Lord,
I keep watch!
If I am not here
who will guard their house?
Watch over their sheep?
Be faithful?
No one but You and I
understands
what faithfulness is.
They call me, "Good dog! Nice dog!"
Words . . .
I take their pats
and the old bones they throw me
and I seem pleased.
They really believe they make me happy.
I take kicks too
when they come my way.
None of that matters.
I keep watch!
Lord,
do not let me die
until, for them,
all danger is driven away.

LUCY NEVER HAD A BONE TO PICK —SHE LOVED UNCONDITIONALLY

Ruth Pollack Coughlin

THE FIRST TIME EVER I saw her face, she was six weeks old. Among her seven sisters and brothers, all of whom gained my attention, she was the only one who, when I picked her up, looked me square in the eye and then nestled her tiny head in the hollow of my neck.

I was sold, and she was for sale. It was 1978. It was December, and I had just turned 35. In New York in those days, I had grown tired of taking care of nothing more than a group of plants. Thriving as they were, those plants, they were not showing a lot of heart, and heart was what I needed.

Twenty-five dollars is what the animal shelter on Long Island told me it would take to liberate this creature, silky and black as India ink and a mixture of at least two breeds, with a minuscule diamond of white on her miraculously small breast. On the way home, in the car I had rented to drive across the bridge and bring us back to Gramercy Park, she curled her body next to mine and rested her face on my right thigh.

It is true that she sighed. It is true that I, a woman without children, attempted to understand that this puppy I had just named Lucy was not a child. It is also true that I could feel my own breast swell, my heart, fluttering, my mind filled with the possibilities of unconditional love — mine for her, hers for me. Unconditional love: It was something I knew most people felt could only be doled out by a mother, even though many therapists acknowledge that family love, especially mother love, can be as polluted as the biggest and the baddest and the nearest toxic dump.

Lucy, in growing up, ate couches. She ate books and records and pillows and eyeglasses. She nibbled at fine Persian rugs. She ate shoes. She believed that the legs of very good chairs were her personal teething rings; she hid her rawhide bones in the pots of those well-tended-to plants, and then she would rediscover those bones quite dramatically, fresh dirt, strewn across varnished hardwood floors. She scratched, and scratched again, at the surfaces of treasured antique chests.

Rolling against a tide of family and friends who castigated me for accepting such bad-dog behavior, I stood firm. She destroys *things*, I said. These thing's are nothing, that's what they are, they're things, they don't live and they don't breathe. She doesn't destroy people. She'll grow out of it, I said. People who destroy people don't ever grow out of it.

And, of course, she grew out of it.

Those who admonished me and never loved Lucy didn't know that for every new couch I bought, that for every pillow or pair of eyeglasses I replaced, I never looked back. They didn't know that Lucy was there during the times about which they knew not.

She was there when I cried, and licked the tears off my face; she was there when I rejoiced, and cavorted around, laughing with me.

She knew what was good and she knew what was bad. When louts were cruel to her, I comforted her; when they were cruel to me, her instinct was such that she curled tighter around me.

Even then, in those early years when the dog-expert books said I should scold her — and I did — she never stopped loving me, nor I her.

No matter what, she would finally smile at me, as only dogs can smile. And always, it would be a smile that went beyond acceptance. It was much more: It was pure. It was without contamination. It was something called love with no baggage, something most therapists would not be able to acknowledge.

Away from the textbooks and the jargon, I was Lucy's god, and she was mine, a statement that has its ironic elements, insofar as I have not yet been able to decide whether there is a god or not.

She and I, transported both in spirit and in body by the

139

man of our dreams, moved from New York to Michigan when she was five.

He grew to love her, as I knew he would, though at first it was slow going. Here was a man who had trained dogs all his life, and then here was Lucy — untrained except in one thing, loving me. He was the one who finally got it, truly got it, because he knew about a kind of love that held no barriers. Because he knew that this bond between Lucy and me was like our marriage. Incontrovertible.

When Lucy got sick on my birthday last month, exactly 13 years after the day I first saw her, I was optimistic.

For more than a dozen years, she had never been ill. Requisite shots, yes. Sickness, no. Romping and yapping and wagging her tail in her own inimitable Lucy way, she was perceived by the mailman, by the Federal Express and the UPS crew as a puppy. She was a dog who slept in the sunshine with her front paws crossed; she was a dog who was at my heels wherever I went.

She was someone who finally showed me the meaning of unconditional love. She was a dog who would never die, I thought, a Lucy who would continue to support me, who would be there, a dog who would see me through the darkest of anyone's worst imagination of what the bleakest days would be like.

We went three times, Lucy and I did, during those two weeks in December, to the veterinarian, surely one of the kindest and most compassionate people I have ever known. She was hospitalized, her heart failing, her kidneys not functioning, an IV unit hooked into her beautifully turned right

TO ABSENT FRIENDS

leg, an inelegant patch marking where her once lustrous black fur had been shaved to accommodate the needle.

The vet allowed me to visit, but not for long, and from a distance. It might upset her to see you, he said, and then he added, if she actually does notice you, it might be disruptive for her to watch you leave. Not wanting to add to the pain she was already in, I peered through a window. She was listless, apparently unaware of my presence.

Maybe she couldn't see me, but she could still smell me, the person with whom she had been sleeping for 13 years, the person who could never tell her enough how much her love was valued. And how I knew, shrinks notwithstanding, that no one could ever get a bead on this, and if they did, they'd probably think it was bonkers and maybe they'd even have to go back to school to figure it out.

This was Lucy who was just barely hanging on, but evidently proud to do even that. My husband and I knew: She was very sick, there would be no recovery. She doesn't, my husband said to me, want to leave you.

Lucy and I went back to the vet.

He allowed me some time alone with her, the vet did, after he told me there would be no turnaround. This was a statement made shortly after the one in which he told me that it had to be my decision. Most people, he said, out of a need that is especially self-serving, prolong the lives of their dying dogs.

I knew what I had to do. Her suffering could not go on, not for another day, not for another hour.

For some time, I held her, I thanked her for being such a

great pal. I kissed her repeatedly, on the top of her head and on her eyes. On her adorable nose and on her incomparable feet. On every part of the small body I had kissed at least a million times during the past 13 years. On her setter-like tail, even though she wasn't a setter, a tail that never stopped wagging.

On her heart that was failing, a heart that had beat so well, so true, a heart that could have, in a split second, taught a legion of therapists what unconditional love is really all about.

The other day, I somehow found the guts to open the envelope with the veterinarian's return address. Euthanasia, the bill said. Fifty dollars.

It seemed to me a small price to pay to allow Lucy, the one who showed me at every turn that she was all heart, to go in peace.

A Dark-Brown Dog

Stephen Crane

A CHILD WAS STANDING on a street-corner. He leaned
with one shoulder against a high board-fence and swayed the
other to and fro, the while kicking carelessly at the gravel.

Sunshine beat upon the cobbles, and a lazy summer
wind raised yellow dust which trailed in clouds down the
avenue. Clattering trucks moved with indistinctness through
it. The child stood dreamily gazing.

After a time, a little dark-brown dog came trotting with
an intent air down the sidewalk. A short rope was dragging
from his neck. Occasionally he trod upon the end of it and
stumbled.

He stopped opposite the child, and the two regarded
each other. The dog hesitated for a moment, but presently he
made some little advances with his tail. The child put out his
hand and called him. In an apologetic manner the dog came
close, and the two had an interchange of friendly partings

and waggles. The dog became more enthusiastic with each moment of the interview, until with his gleeful caperings he threatened to overturn the child. Whereupon the child lifted his hand and struck the dog a blow upon the head.

This thing seemed to overpower and astonish the little dark-brown dog, and wounded him to the heart. He sank down in despair at the child's feet. When the blow was repeated, together with an admonition in childish sentences, he turned over upon his back, and held his paws in a peculiar manner. At the same time with his ears and his eyes he offered a small prayer to the child.

He looked so comical on his back, and holding his paws peculiarly, that the child was greatly amused and gave him little taps repeatedly, to keep him so. But the little dark-brown dog took this chastisement in the most serious way, and no doubt considered that he had committed some grave crime, for he wriggled contritely and showed his repentance in every way that was in his power. He pleaded with the child and petitioned him, and offered more prayers.

At last the child grew weary of this amusement and turned toward home. The dog was praying at the time. He lay on his back and turned his eyes upon the retreating form.

Presently he struggled to his feet and started after the child. The latter wandered in a perfunctory way toward his home, stopping at times to investigate various matters. During one of these pauses he discovered the little dark-brown dog who was following him with the air of a footpad.

The child beat his pursuer with a small stick he had found. The dog lay down and prayed until the child had finished, and resumed his journey. Then he scrambled erect and took up pursuit again.

On the way to his home the child turned many times and beat the dog, proclaiming with childish gestures that he held him in contempt as an unimportant dog, with no value save for a moment. For being this quality of animal the dog apologized and eloquently expressed regret, but he continued stealthily to follow the child. His manner grew so very guilty that he slunk like an assassin.

When the child reached his door-step, the dog was industriously ambling a few yards in the rear. He became so agitated with shame when he again confronted the child that he forgot the dragging rope. He tripped upon it and fell forward.

The child sat down on the step and the two had another interview. During it the dog greatly exerted himself to please the child. He performed a few gambols with such abandon that the child suddenly saw him to be a valuable thing. He made a swift, avaricious charge and seized the rope.

He dragged his captive into a hall and up many long stairways in a dark tenement. The dog made willing efforts, but he could not hobble very skillfully up the stairs because he was very small and soft, and at last the pace of the engrossed child grew so energetic that the dog became panic-stricken. In his mind he was being dragged toward a grim unknown. His eyes grew wild with the terror of it. He began to wiggle his head frantically and to brace his legs.

The child redoubled his exertions. They had a battle on the stairs. The child was victorious because he was com-

pletely absorbed in his purpose, and because the dog was
very small. He dragged his acquirement to the door of his
home, and finally with triumph across the threshold.

No one was in. The child sat down on the floor and
made overtures to the dog. These the dog instantly accepted.
He beamed with affection upon his new friend. In a short
time they were firm and abiding comrades.

When the child's family appeared, they made a great row.
The dog was examined and commented upon and called
names. Scorn was leveled at him from all eyes, so that he
became much embarrassed and drooped like a scorched
plant. But the child went sturdily to the center of the floor,
and, at the top of his voice, championed the dog. It happened that he was roaring protestations, with his arms
clasped about the dog's neck, when the father of the family
came in from work.

The parent demanded to know what the blazes they were
making the kid howl for. It was explained in many words
that the infernal kid wanted to introduce a disreputable dog
into the family.

A family council was held. On this depended the dog's
fate, but he in no way heeded, being busily engaged in chewing the end of the child's dress.

The affair was quickly ended. The father of the family, it
appears, was in a particularly savage temper that evening and
when he perceived that it would amaze and anger everybody
if such a dog were allowed to remain, he decided that it
should be so. The child, crying softly, took his friend off to a
retired part of the room to hobnob with him, while the

father quelled a fierce rebellion of his wife. So it came to pass that the dog was a member of the household.

He and the child were associated together at all times save when the child slept. The child became a guardian and a friend. If the large folk kicked the dog and threw things at him, the child made loud and violent objections. Once when the child had run, protesting loudly, with tears raining down his face and his arms outstretched, to protect his friend, he had been struck in the head with a very large saucepan from the hand of his father, enraged at some seeming lack of courtesy in the dog. Ever after, the family were careful how they threw things at the dog. Moreover, the latter grew very skillful in avoiding missiles and feet. In a small room containing a stove, a table, a bureau and some chairs, he would display strategic ability of a high order, dodging, feinting and scuttling about among the furniture. He could force three or four people armed with brooms, sticks and handfuls of coal, to use all their ingenuity to get in a blow. And even when they did, it was seldom that they could do him a serious injury or leave any imprint.

But when the child was present, these scenes did not occur. It came to be recognized that if the dog was molested, the child would burst into sobs, and as the child, when started, was very riotous and practically unquenchable, the dog had therein a safeguard.

However, the child could not always be near. At night, when he was asleep, his dark-brown friend would raise from some black corner a wild, wailful cry, a song of infinite lowliness and despair, that would go shuddering and sobbing among the buildings of the block and cause people to swear. At these times the singer would often be chased all over the kitchen and hit with a great variety of articles.

Sometimes, too, the child himself used to beat the dog, although it is not known that he ever had what could be truly called a just cause. The dog always accepted these thrashings with an air of admitted guilt. He was too much of a dog to try to look to be a martyr or to plot revenge. He received the blows with deep humility, and furthermore he forgave his friend the moment the child had finished, and was ready to caress the child's hand with his little red tongue.

When misfortune came upon the child, and his troubles overwhelmed him, he would often crawl under the table and lay his small distressed head on the dog's back. The dog was ever sympathetic. It is not to be supposed that at such times he took occasion to refer to the unjust beatings his friend, when provoked, had administered to him.

He did not achieve any notable degree of intimacy with the other members of the family. He had no confidence in them, and the fear that he would express at their casual approach often exasperated them exceedingly. They used to gain a certain satisfaction in underfeeding him, but finally his friend the child grew to watch the matter with some care, and when he forgot it, the dog was often successful in secret for himself.

So the dog prospered. He developed a large bark, which came wondrously from such a small rug of a dog. He ceased to howl persistently at night. Sometimes, indeed, in his sleep, he would utter little yells, as from pain, but that occurred, no doubt, when in his dreams he encountered huge flaming dogs who threatened him direfully.

His devotion to the child grew until it was a sublime thing. He wagged at his approach; he sank down in despair at his departure. He could detect the sound of the child's step among all the noises of the neighborhood. It was like a calling voice to him.

The scene of their companionship was a kingdom governed by this terrible potentate, the child; but neither criticism nor rebellion ever lived for an instant in the heart of the one subject. Down in the mystic, hidden fields of his little dog-soul bloomed flowers of love and fidelity and perfect faith.

The child was in the habit of going on many expeditions to observe strange things in the vicinity. On these occasions his friend usually jogged aimfully along behind. Perhaps, though, he went ahead. This necessitated his turning around every quarter-minute to make sure the child was coming. He was filled with a large idea of the importance of these journeys. He would carry himself with such an air! He was proud to be the retainer of so great a monarch.

One day, however, the father of the family got quite exceptionally drunk. He came home and held carnival with the cooking utensils, the furniture and his wife. He was in the midst of this recreation when the child, followed by the dark-brown dog, entered the room. They were returning from their voyages.

The child's practiced eye instantly noted his father's state. He dived under the table, where experience had taught him was a rather safe place. The dog, lacking skill in such matters, was, of course, unaware of the true condition of affairs. He looked with interested eyes at his friend's sudden dive. He interpreted it to mean: Joyous gambol. He started to patter across the floor to join him. He was the picture of a little dark-brown dog en route to a friend.

The head of the family saw him at this moment. He gave a huge howl of joy, and knocked the dog down with a heavy coffee-pot. The dog, yelling in supreme astonishment and fear, writhed to his feet and ran for cover. The man kicked out with a ponderous foot. It caused the dog to swerve as if caught in a tide. A second blow of the coffee-pot laid him upon the floor.

Here the child, uttering loud cries, came valiantly forth like a knight. The father of the family paid no attention to these calls of the child, but advanced with glee upon the dog. Upon being knocked down twice in swift succession, the latter apparently gave up all hope of escape. He rolled over on his back and held his paws in a peculiar manner. At the same time with his eyes and his ears he offered up a small prayer.

But the father was in a mood for having fun, and it occurred to him that it would be a fine thing to throw the dog out of the window. So he reached down and grabbing the animal by a leg, lifted him, squirming, up. He swung him two or three times hilariously about his head, and then flung him with great accuracy through the window.

The soaring dog created a surprise in the block. A woman watering plants in an opposite window gave an involuntary shout and dropped a flower-pot. A man in another window leaned perilously out to watch the flight of the dog. A woman who had been hanging out clothes in a yard, began to caper wildly. Her mouth was filled with clothes-pins, but her arms gave vent to a sort of exclamation. In appearance she was like a gagged prisoner. Children ran whooping.

The dark-brown body crashed in a heap on the roof of a shed five stories below. From thence it rolled to the pavement of an alleyway.

The child in the room far above burst into a long, dirge-like cry, and toddled hastily out of the room. It took him a long time to reach the alley, because his size compelled him to go downstairs backward, one step at a time, and holding with both hands to the step above.

When they came for him later, they found him seated by the body of his dark-brown friend.

THE DOG THAT BIT PEOPLE

James Thurber

PROBABLY NO ONE MAN should have as many dogs in his
life as I have had, but there was more pleasure than distress
in them for me except in the case of an Airedale named
Muggs. He gave me more trouble than all the other fifty-
four or -five put together, although my moment of keenest
embarrassment was the time a Scotch terrier named Jeannie,
who had just had six puppies in the clothes closet of a
fourth-floor apartment in New York, had the unexpected
seventh and last at the corner of Eleventh Street and Fifth
Avenue during a walk she had insisted on taking. Then, too,
there was the prize-winning French poodle, a great big black
poodle — none of your little, untroublesome white minia-
tures — who got sick riding in the rumble seat of a car with
me on her way to the Greenwich Dog Show. She had a red
rubber bib tucked around her throat and, since a rain storm
came up when we were halfway through the Bronx, I had to

hold over her a small green umbrella, really more of a para-
sol. The rain beat down fearfully and suddenly the driver of
the car drove into a big garage, filled with mechanics. It
happened so quickly that I forgot to put the umbrella down
and I will always remember, with sickening distress, the look
of incredulity mixed with hatred that came over the face of
the particular hardened garage man that came over to see
what we wanted, when he took a look at me and the poodle. All garage men, and people of that intolerant stripe,
hate poodles with their curious haircut, especially with
pom-poms that you got to leave on their hips if you expect
the dog to win a prize.

But the Airdale, as I have said, was the worst of all my
dogs. He really wasn't my dog, as a matter of fact: I came
home from a vacation one summer to find that my brother
Roy had bought him while I was away. A big, burly, choleric
dog, he always acted as if he thought I wasn't one of the family. There was a slight advantage in being one of the family,
for he didn't bite the family as often as he bit strangers. Still,
in the years that we had him he bit everybody but mother,
and he made a pass at her once but missed. That was during
the month when we suddenly had mice, and Muggs refused
to do anything about them. Nobody ever had mice exactly
like the mice we had that month. They acted like pet mice,
almost like mice somebody had trained. They were so
friendly that one night when mother entertained at dinner
the Friraliras, a club she and my father had belonged to for
twenty years, she put down a lot of dishes with food in them
on the pantry floor so that the mice would be satisfied with

that and wouldn't come into the dining room. Muggs stayed out in the pantry with the mice, lying on the floor, growling to himself — not at the mice, but about all the people in the next room that he would have liked to get at. Mother slipped out into the pantry once to see how everything was going. Everything was going fine. It made her so mad to see Muggs lying there, oblivious of the mice — they came running up to her — that she slapped him and he slashed at her, but didn't make it. He was sorry immediately, mother said. He was always sorry, she said, after he bit someone, but we could not understand how she figured this out. He didn't act sorry.

Mother used to send a box of candy every Christmas to the people the Airedale bit. The list finally contained forty or more names. Nobody could understand why we didn't get rid of the dog. I didn't understand it very well myself, but we didn't get rid of him. I think that one or two people tried to poison Muggs — he acted poisoned once in a while — and old Major Moberly fired at him once with his service revolver near the Seneca Hotel in East Broad Street — but Muggs lived to be almost eleven years old and even when he could hardly get around he bit a congressman who had called to see my father on business. My mother had never liked the congressman — she said the signs of his horoscope showed he couldn't be trusted (he was Saturn with the moon in Virgo) — but she sent him a box of candy that Christmas. He sent it right back, probably because he suspected it was trick candy. Mother persuaded herself it was all for the best that the dog had bitten him, even though father lost an important business association because of it. "I wouldn't be associated with such a man," mother said, "Muggs could read him like a book."

We used to take turns feeding Muggs to be on his good side, but that didn't always work. He was never in a very good humor, even after a meal. Nobody knew exactly what was the matter with him, but whatever it was it made him irascible, especially in the mornings. Roy never felt very well in the morning, either, especially before breakfast, and once when he came downstairs and found that Muggs had moodily chewed up the morning paper he hit him in the face with a grapefruit and then jumped up on the dining room table, scattering dishes and silverware and spilling the coffee. Muggs' first free leap carried him all the way across the table and into a brass fire screen in front of the gas grate but he was back on his feet in a moment and in the end he got Roy and gave him a pretty vicious bite in the leg. Then he was all over it; he never bit anyone more than once at a time. Mother always mentioned that as an argument in his favor; she said he had a quick temper but that he didn't hold a grudge. She was forever defending him. I think she liked him because he wasn't well. "He's not strong," she would say, pityingly, but that was inaccurate; he may not have been well but he was terribly strong.

One time my mother went to the Chittenden Hotel to call on a woman mental healer who was lecturing in Columbus on the subject of "Harmonious Vibrations." She wanted to find out if it was possible to get harmonious vibrations into a dog. "He's a large tan-colored Airedale," mother explained. The woman said that she had never treated a dog but she advised my mother to hold the thought that he did not bite and would not bite. Mother was holding the thought the very next morning when Muggs got the iceman but she blamed that slip-up on the iceman. "If you didn't think he would bite you, he wouldn't," mother told him. He stomped out of the house in a terrible jangle of vibrations.

One morning when Muggs bit me slightly, more or less in passing, I reached down and grabbed his short stumpy tail and hoisted him into the air. It was a foolhardy thing to do and the last time I saw my mother, about six months ago, she said she didn't know what possessed me. I don't either, except that I was pretty mad. As long as I held the dog off the floor by his tail he couldn't get at me, but he twisted and jerked so, snarling all the time, that I realized I couldn't hold him that way very long. I carried him to the kitchen and flung him onto the floor and shut the door on him just as he crashed against it. But I forgot about the backstairs. Muggs went up the backstairs and down the frontstairs and had me cornered in the living room. I managed to get up onto the mantelpiece above the fireplace, but it gave way and came down with a tremendous crash throwing a large marble clock, several vases, and myself heavily to the floor. Muggs was so alarmed by the racket that when I picked myself up he had disappeared. We couldn't find him anywhere, although we whistled and shouted, until old Mrs. Detweiler called after dinner that night. Muggs had bitten her once, in the leg, and she came into the living room only after we assured her that Muggs had run away. She had just seated herself when, with a great growling and scratching of claws,

Muggs emerged from under a davenport where he had been quietly hiding all the time, and bit her again. Mother examined the bite and put arnica on it and told Mrs. Detweiler that it was only a bruise. "He just bumped you," she said. But Mrs. Detweiler left the house in a nasty state of mind.

Lots of people reported our Airedale to the police but my father held a municipal office at the time and was on friendly terms with the police. Even so, the cops had been out a couple of times — once when Muggs bit Mrs. Rufus Sturtevant and again when he bit Lieutenant-Governor Malloy — but mother told them that it hadn't been Muggs' fault but the fault of the people who were bitten. "When he starts for them, they scream," she explained, "and that excites him." The cops suggested that it might be a good idea to tie the dog up, but mother said that it mortified him to be tied up and that he wouldn't eat when he was tied up.

Muggs at his meals was an unusual sight. Because of the fact that if you reached toward the floor he would bite you, we usually put his food plate on top of an old kitchen table with a bench alongside the table. Muggs would stand on the bench and eat. I remember that my mother's Uncle Horatio, who boasted that he was the third man up Missionary Ridge, was splutteringly indignant when he found out that we fed the dog on a table beause we were all afraid to put his plate on the floor. He said he wasn't afraid of any dog that ever lived and that he would put the dog's plate on the floor if we would give it to him. Roy said that if Uncle Horatio had fed Muggs on the ground just before the battle he would have been the first man up Missionary Ridge. Uncle Horatio was furious "Bring him in! Bring him in now!" he shouted. "I'll feed the —————— on the floor!" Roy was all for giving him a chance, but my father wouldn't hear of it. He said that Muggs had already been fed. "I'll feed him again!" bawled Uncle Horatio. We had quite a time quieting him.

In his last year Muggs used to spend practically all of his time outdoors. He didn't like to stay in the house for some reason or other — perhaps it held too many unpleasant memories for him. Anyway, it was hard to get him to come in and as a result the garbage man, the iceman and the laundry man wouldn't come near the house. We had to haul the garbage down to the corner, take the laundry out and bring it back, and meet the iceman a block from home. After this had gone on for some time we hit on an ingenious arrangement for getting the dog in the house so that we could lock him up while the gas meter was read, and so on. Muggs was afraid of only one thing, an electrical storm. Thunder and lightning frightened him out of his senses (I think he thought a storm had broken the day the mantelpiece fell). He would rush into the house and hide under a bed or in a clothes closet. So we fixed up a thunder machine out of a long narrow piece of sheet iron with a wooden handle on one end. Mother would shake this vigorously when she wanted to get Muggs into the house. It made an excellent imitation of thunder, but I suppose it was the most roundabout system for running a household that was ever devised. It took a lot out of mother.

A few months before Muggs died, he got to "seeing things." He would rise slowly from the floor, growling low, and stalk stiff-legged and menacing toward nothing at all. Sometimes the Thing would be just a little to the right or left of a visitor. Once a Fuller Brush salesman got hysterics. Muggs came wandering into the room like Hamlet following his father's ghost. His eyes were fixed on a spot just to the left of the Fuller Brush man, who stood it until Muggs was about three slow, creeping paces from him. Then he shouted. Muggs wavered on pass him into the hallway grumbling to himself but the Fuller man went on shouting. I think mother had to throw a pan of cold water on him before he stopped.

That was the way she used to stop us boys when we got into fights.

Muggs died quite suddenly one night. Mother wanted to bury him in the family lot under a marble stone with some such inscription as "Flights of angels sing thee to they rest" but we persuaded her it was against the law. In the end we just put up a smooth board above his grave along a lonely road. On the board I wrote with an indelible pencil "Cave Canem." Mother was quite pleased with the simple classic dignity of the old Latin epitaph.

COWBOYS, GENERALLY SPEAKING

Sunny Hancock

You know, I always did work for big outfits
Even way back when I was a pup.
In fact, when I first got started
I was still sort of gettin' growed up.

They hired cowboys to handle their livestock
And to ride out those rimrocks and bogs.
I seen lots of men working cattle,
But I never did see any dogs.

Then old age started creepin' up on me
And I want to tell you the truth.
The wrecks and the spills kinda caught up with me
That I'd taken back there in my youth.

I was tired of them tough old hard winters,
And them long seventeen-hour days
Ridin' them cranky old horses
Plus the way that those cow outfits pays.

Well, we'd saved up a couple of pesos,
So we took out a hell of a loan,
And me and my wife and a couple of banks
Bought a little old place of our own.

'Course, we all know there isn't much cow work
On them "Farmer John" outfits at all,
just a couple of days in the springtime,
And then three or four more in the fall.

And the rest of the time, why, you're farmin'
Or fencin', or puffin' up hay,
Or a-wrenchin' some greasy old tractor,
That's enough to make anyone's day.

For the help that you get at your brandin'
And for all of your cowpunchin' labors,
Why, you just go and get on the old telephone,
And you call up a bunch of your neighbors.

So early and bright the next mornin'
They'll start showin' up there, of course,
And they'll all have at least three good cow dogs
In the trailer, and sometimes, a horse.

I'd heard 'em all talk of these cow dogs,
How in pasture, in feedlot, or pen
Each one was a surefire replacement,
For at least half a dozen good men.

I don't want to say they was lying,
'Cause that would be awfully uncouth,
But I stand here this evenin' to tell you
They sure kicked hell outa the truth.

These dogs was all runnin' and barkin',
just causin' confusion, of course.
If one wasn't parked on his butt in the gate
Why, the bastard was heelin' your horse.

The cows was all fightin' these pot hounds
And then if a calf should run back,
Why some old dog would "yowp" out the signal
And they'd build to him all in a pack.

And they'd run him plumb out of the country
Or at least 'till he gave out and lay down,
Then they'd come back a-grinnin' and waggin' their tails
Like they'd just been named Grand Champion Hound.

These dogs came in all colors and sizes.
Those old boys sure knew how to pick 'em.
They all thought "Come back here, you dumb SOB."
Meant exactly the same thing as "Sic 'em."

But one dog stood out from his brothers
Like a hawk with the hens in the yard.
He was ten times as dumb as the others;
It was Barney's old dog he called Pard.

I'm not gonna go into detail,
But if old Pard had of fell in the creek,
A man with a five gallon bucket
Could have stood and skimmed "dumb" for a week.

And old Barney would holler and cuss him,
Call him names that I dassn't to mention.
But old Pard just kept on a-doin' his thing
And he'd not pay one bit of attention.

But then somthin' happened that August
I took as a stroke of good luck.
Pard was chasin' a Rabbit (the Volkswagen kind)
And got hit by a Peterbuilt truck.

That's been just three years here this summer
And I wanna tell you the truth.
It ain't like old Pard ain't been missed some
'Cause he has, about like a sore tooth.

Just last week, why, I went to a brandin'
Down there at old Joe Dancer's place.
At noon, why, we all was a-standin
'Round washin' our hands and our face.

A new feller had moved into the valley.
We're all BS'n there in the yard
When I heard Barney tellin' this new guy
'Bout this old cowdog he once had named Pard.

Seems like this old dog could speak seventeen languages;
He never done nothin' by half.
And he always knew right to the letter
What an old cow was a-tellin' her calf.

He could sort out the steers from the heifers
And just ask any of these fellers here.
I'd rather had Pard than three or four men
If I had to hold up a rodeer.

He'd work "ins," and the "byes" down an alley
You might have seen some of that kind.
But in order to get a dog workin' like that,
Why, you sure gotta make that dog mind.

I stood there completely dumbfounded
My mind in a terrible fog.
I couldn't believe me and Barney
Was a-thinkin' about the same dog.

Then a thought hit me over the eyebrow
And rolled around under my hat.
I could think of a lot of old fellers
That remembered their horses like that.

But time heals all wounds, so they tell me,
And changes the memories of men.
You don't see things just like they happened,
But more like you wish they'd have been.

So just for the record I'll tell you,
The lowdown on cowdogs, it's said,
They ain't worth a flip when they're livin'
But they're good SOBs when they're dead!

TROUBLE

Gene Hill

WE LOST A LITTLE PUPPY the other day to a speeding car. And a lot of the magic has disappeared from the kitchen where she ruled the roost. Whoever said "you can't buy happiness" forgot little puppies. "Trouble" was a tiny package crammed to overflowing with mischief, charm, excitement, curiosity and affection. She scattered love around our house the way the wind scatters leaves. The empty voids in space are not one whit more vast than the little corner by the stove where the puppy slept — when the puppy's sleeping somewhere else forever.

DO DOGS HAVE SOULS?

James Herriot

THE CARD DANGLED ABOVE the old lady's bed. It read
'God is Near' but it wasn't like the usual religious text; It did-
n't have a frame or ornate printing. It was just a strip of cardboard about eight inches long with plain lettering which
might have said 'No smoking' or 'Exit' and it was looped
carelessly over an old gas bracket so that Miss Stubbs from
where she lay could look up at it and read "God is Near" in
square black capitals.

There wasn't much more Miss Stubbs could see; perhaps
a few feet of privet hedge through the frayed curtains but
mainly it was just the cluttered little room which had been
her world for so many years.

The room was on the ground floor and in front of the
cottage, and as I came up through the wilderness which had
once been a garden I could see the dogs watching me from
where they had jumped on to the old lady's bed, And when I

knocked on the door the place almost erupted with their barking. It was always like this. I had been visiting regularly for over a year and the pattern never changed; the furious barking, then Mrs. Broadwith who looked after Miss Stubbs would push all the animals but my patient into the back kitchen and open the door and I would go in and see Miss Stubbs in the corner in her bed with the card hanging over it.

She had been there for a long time and would never get up again. But she never mentioned her illness and pain to me; all her concern was for her three dogs and two cats.

Today it was old Prince and I was worried about him. It was his heart — just about the most spectacular valvular incompetence I had ever heard. He was waiting for me as I came in, pleased as ever to see me, his long, fringed tail waving gently.

The sight of that tail used to make me think there must be a lot of Irish Setter in Prince but I was inclined to change my mind as I worked my way forward over the bulging black and white body to the shaggy head and upstanding Alsatian ears. Miss Stubbs often used to call him 'Mr. Heinz' and though he may not have had 57 varieties in him his hybrid vigour had stood him in good stead. With his heart he should have been dead long ago.

"I thought I'd best give you a ring, Mr. Herriot," Mrs. Broadwith said. She was a comfortable, elderly widow with a square, ruddy face contrasting sharply with the pinched features on the pillow. "He's been coughing right bad this week and this morning he was a bit staggery, Still eats well, though."

"I bet he does." I ran my hands over the rolls of fat on

the ribs. "It would take something really drastic to put old Prince off his grub."

Miss Stubbs laughed from the bed and the old dog, his mouth wide, eyes dancing, seemed to be joining in the joke. I put my stethoscope over his heart and listened, knowing well what I was going to hear. They say the heart is supposed to go 'Lub-dup, lub-dup', but Prince's went 'swish-swoosh, swish-swoosh'. There seemed to be nearly as much blood leaking back as was being pumped into the circulatory system. And another thing, the 'swish-swoosh' was a good bit faster than last time; he was on oral digitalis but it wasn't quite doing its job.

Gloomily I moved the stethoscope over the rest of the chest. Like all old dogs with a chronic heart weakness he had an ever-present bronchitis and I listened without enthusiasm to the symphony of whistles, rales, squeaks and bubbles which signalled the workings of Prince's lungs. The old dog stood very erect and proud, his tail still waving slowly. He always took it as a tremendous compliment when I examined him and there was no doubt he was enjoying himself now. Fortunately his was not a very painful ailment.

Straightening up, I patted his head and he responded immediately by trying to put his paws on my chest. He didn't quite make it and even that slight exertion started his ribs heaving and his tongue lolling. I gave him an intramuscular injection and another of morphine hydrochloride which he accepted with apparent pleasure as part of the game.

"I hope that will steady his heart and breathing, Miss Stubbs. You'll find he'll be a bit dopey for the rest of the day and that will help, too. Carry on with the tablets, and I'm going to leave you some more medicine for his bronchitis." I handed over a bottle of my old standby mixture of ipecacuanha and ammonium acetate.

The next stage of the visit began now as Mrs. Broadwith brought in a cup of tea and the rest of the animals were let out of the kitchen. There were Ben, a Sealyham, and Sally, a Cocker Spaniel, and they started a deafening barking contest with Prince. They were closely followed by the cats, Arthur and Susie, who stalked in gracefully and began to rub themselves against my trouser legs.

It was the usual scenario for the many cups of tea I had drunk with Miss Stubbs under the little card which dangled above her bed.

"How are you today?" I asked.

"Oh, much better," she replied and immediately, as always, changed the subject.

Mostly she liked to talk about her pets and the ones she had known right back to her girlhood. She spoke a lot, too, about the days when her family were alive. She loved to describe the escapades of her three brothers and today she showed me a photograph which Mrs. Broadwith had found at the bottom of a drawer.

I took it from her and three young men in the knee breeches and little round caps of the nineties smiled up at me from the yellowed old print; they all held long church warden pipes and the impish humour in their expressions came down undimmed over the years.

"My word, they look really bright lads, Miss Stubbs," I said.

"Oh, they were young rips!" she exclaimed. She threw back her head and laughed and for a moment her face was radiant, transfigured by her memories.

The things I had heard in the village came back to me; about the prosperous father and his family who lived in the big house many years ago. Then the foreign investments which crashed and the sudden change in circumstances. "When t'owd feller died he was about skint," one old man had said. "There's not much brass there now."

Probably just enough brass to keep Miss Stubbs and her animals alive and to pay Mrs Broadwith. Not enough to keep the garden dug or the house painted or for any of the normal little luxuries.

And, sitting there, drinking my tea, with the dogs in a row by the bedside and the cats making themselves comfortable on the bed itself, I felt as I had often felt before — a bit afraid of the responsibility I had. The one thing which brought some light into the life of the brave old woman was the transparent devotion of this shaggy bunch whose eyes were never far from her face. And the snag was that they were all elderly.

There had, in fact, been four dogs originally, but one of them, a truly ancient golden Labrador, had died a few months previously. And now I had the rest of them to look after and none of them less than ten years old.

They were perky enough but all showing some of the signs of old age; Prince with his heart, Sally, beginning to drink a lot of water which made me wonder if she was starting with a pyometra, Ben growing steadily thinner with his

173
TO ABSENT FRIENDS

nephritis. I couldn't give him new kidneys and I hadn't much faith in the hexamine tablets I had prescribed. Another peculiar thing about Ben was that I was always having to clip his claws; they grew at an extraordinary rate.

The cats were better, though Susie was a bit scraggy and I kept up a morbid kneading of her furry abdomen for signs of lymphosarcoma. Arthur was the best of the bunch; he never seemed to ail anything beyond a tendency for his teeth to tartar up.

This must have been in Miss Stubbs' mind because, when I had finished my tea, she asked me to look at him. I hauled him across the bedspread and opened his mouth.

"Yes, there's a bit of the old trouble there. Might as well fix it while I'm here."

Arthur was a huge, grey, neutered Tom, a living denial of all those theories that cats are cold-natured, selfish and the rest. His fine eyes, framed in the widest cat face I have ever seen, looked out on the world with an all-embracing benevolence and tolerance. His every movement was marked by immense dignity.

As I started to scrape his teeth his chest echoed with a booming purr like a distant outboard motor. There was no need for anybody to hold him; he sat there placidly and moved only once — when I was using forceps to crack off a tough piece of tartar from a back tooth and accidentally nicked his gum. He casually raised a massive paw as if to say 'Have a care, chum,' but his claws were sheathed.

My next visit was less than a month later and was in response to an urgent summons from Mrs Broadwith at six o'clock in the evening. Ben had collapsed. I jumped straight into my car and in less than ten minutes was threading my way through the overgrown grass in the front garden with the animals watching from their window. The barking broke out as I knocked, but Ben's was absent. As I went into the little room I saw the old dog lying on his side, very still, by the bed.

D.O.A. is what we write in the day book. Dead on arrival. Just three words but they covered all kinds of situations — the end of milk fever cows, bloated bullocks, calves in fits. And tonight they meant that I wouldn't be clipping old Ben's claws any more.

It wasn't often these nephritis cases went off so suddenly but his urine albumen had been building up dangerously lately.

"Well, it was quick, Miss Stubbs. I'm sure the old chap didn't suffer at all." My words sounded lame and ineffectual.

The old lady was in full command of herself. No tears, only a fixity of expression as she looked down from the bed at her companion for so many years. My idea was to get him out of the place as quickly as possible and I pulled a blanket under him and lifted him up. As I was moving away, Miss Stubbs said, "Wait a moment." With an effort she turned on to her side and gazed at Ben. Still without changing expression, she reached out and touched his head lightly. Then she lay back calmly as I hurried from the room.

In the back kitchen I had a whispered conference with Mrs Broadwith. "I'll run down t'village and get Fred Manners to come and bury him," she said. "And if you've got time could you stay with the old lady while I'm gone. Talk to her, like, it'll do her good."

I went back and sat down by the bed. Miss Stubbs looked out of the window for a few moments then turned to me. "You know, Mr Herriot." she said casually. "It will be my turn next."

"What do you mean?"

"Well, tonight Ben has gone and I'm going to be the next one. I just know it."

"Oh, nonsense! You're feeling a bit low, that's all. We all do when this happens." But I was disturbed. I had never heard her even hint at such a thing before.

"I'm not afraid," she said. "I know there's something better waiting for me. I've never had any doubts." There was silence between us as she lay calmly looking up at the card on the gas bracket.

Then the head on the pillow turned to me again. "I have only one fear." Her expression changed with startling suddenness as if a mask had dropped. The brave face was almost unrecognizable. A kind of terror flickered in her eyes and she quickly grasped my hand.

"It's my dogs and cats, Mr Herriot. I'm afraid I might never see them when I'm gone and it worries me so. You see, I know I'll be reunited with my parents and my brothers but... but ..."

"Well, why not with your animals?"

"That's just it." She rocked her head on the pillow and for the first time I saw tears on her cheeks. "They say animals have no souls."

"Who says?"

"Oh, I've read it and I know a lot of religious people believe it."

"Well I don't believe it." I patted the hand which still grasped mine. "If having a soul means being able to feel love and loyalty and gratitude, then animals are better off than a lot of humans. You've nothing to worry about there."

"Oh, I hope you're right. Sometimes I lie at night thinking about it."

"I know I'm right, Miss Stubbs, and don't you argue with me. They teach us vets all about animals' souls."

The tension left her face and she laughed with a return of her old spirit. "I'm sorry to bore you with this and I'm not going to talk about it again. But before you go, I warn you to be absolutely honest with me. I don't want reassurance from you — just the truth. I know you are very young but please tell me — what are your beliefs? Will my animals go with me?"

She stared intently into my eyes. I shifted in my chair and swallowed once or twice.

"Miss Stubbs, I'm afraid I'm a bit foggy about all this," I said. "But I'm absolutely certain of one thing. Wherever you are going, they are going too."

She still stared at me but her face was calm again. "Thank you, Mr Herriot. I know you are being honest with me. That is what you really believe, isn't it?"

"I do believe it," I said. "With all my heart I believe it."

It must have been about a month later and it was entirely by accident that I learned I had seen Miss Stubbs for the last time. When a lonely, penniless old woman dies people don't rush up to you on the street to tell you. I was on my rounds and a farmer happened to mention that the cottage in Corby village was up for sale.

"But what about Miss Stubbs?" I asked.

"Oh, went off sudden about three weeks ago. House is in a bad state, they say — nowt been done at it for years."

"Mrs Broadwith isn't staying on, then?"

"Nay, I hear she's staying at t'other end of village."

"Do you know what's happened to the dogs and cats?"

"What dogs and cats?"

I cut my visit short. And I didn't go straight home though it was nearly lunch time. Instead I urged my complaining little car at top speed to Corby and asked the first person I saw where Mrs Broadwith was living. It was a tiny house but attractive and Mrs Broadwith answered my knock herself.

"'Oh, come in, Mr Herriot. It's right good of you to call." I went inside and we sat facing each other across a scrubbed table top.

"Well, it was sad about the old lady," she said.

"Yes I've only just heard."

"Any road, she had a peaceful end. Just slept away at finish."

"I'm glad to hear that."

Mrs Broadwith looked round the room. "I was real lucky to get this place — it's just what I've always wanted."

I could contain myself no longer. "What's happened to the animals?" I blurted out.

"Oh, they're in t'garden", she said calmly. "I've got a grand big stretch at back." She got up and opened the door and with a surge of relief I watched my old friends pour in.

Arthur was on my knee in a flash, arching himself ecstatically against my arm while his outboard motor roared softly above the barking of the dogs. Prince, wheezy as ever, tail fanning the air, laughed up at me delightedly between barks.

"They look great, Mrs Broadwith. How long are they going to be here?"

"They're here for good. I think just as much about them as t'old lady ever did and I couldn't be parted from them. They'll have a good home with me as long as they live."

I looked at the typical Yorkshire country face, at the heavy cheeks with their grim lines delied by the kindly eyes. "This is wonderful," I said. "But won't you find it just a bit... er... expensive to feed them?"

"Nay, you don't have to worry about that. I've a bit put away."

"Well fine, fine, and I'll be looking in now and then to see how they are. I'm through the village every few days." I got up and started for the door.

Mrs. Broadwith held up her hand. "There's just one thing I'd like you to do before they start selling off the things at the cottage. Would you please pop in and collect what's left of your medicines. They're in t'front room."

I took the key and drove along to the other end of the village. As I pushed open the rickety gate and began to walk through the tangled grass the front of the cottage looked strangley lifeless without the faces of the dogs at the window; and when the door creaked open and I went inside the silence was like a heavy pall.

Nothing had been moved. The bed with its rumpled

blankets was still in the corner. I moved around, picking up half empty bottles, a jar of ointment, the cardboard box with old Ben's tablets — a lot of good they had done him.

When I had got everything I looked slowly round the little room. I wouldn't be coming here any more and at the door I paused and read for the last time the card which hung over the bed.

QUATRAIN

George Crabbe

With eye upraised, his master's look to scan,
    The joy, the solace, and the aid of man;
The rich man's guardian, and the poor man's friend,
    The only creature faithful to the end.

Excerpt from

MIDNIGHT IN THE GARDEN OF GOOD AND EVIL

John Berendt

IF I HAPPENED TO BE walking along Bull Street in the late afternoon I would invariably see a very old and very dignified black man. He always wore a suit and tie, a starched white shirt, and a fedora. His ties were muted paisleys and regimental stripes, and his suits were fine and well tailored, though apparently made for a slightly larger person.

Every day at the same time, the old man walked through the cast-iron gates of the grandiose Armstrong House at the north end of Forsyth Park. He turned left and proceeded up Bull Street all the way to City Hall and back. He was very much a gentleman. He tipped his hat and bowed in greeting. But I noticed that he and the people he spoke with — usually well-dressed businessmen — played a very odd game. The men would ask him, "Still walking the dog?" It was perfectly clear that the old man was not walking a dog, but he would respond by saying, "Oh, yes. Still walking the dog." Then he would look over his shoulder and say to the air behind him, "Come on, Patrick!" And off he would go.

One day, as I came through Madison Square, I saw him standing by the monument facing a semicircle of tourists. He was singing. I could not make out the words, but I could hear his reedy tenor voice. The tourists applauded when he was done, and one of the lady tour guides slipped something into his hand. He bowed and left them. We approached the crosswalk at the same time.

"That was very nice." I said.

"Why, thank you kindly," he replied in his courtly way. "My name is William Simon Glover."

I introduced myself and told Mr. Glover that it seemed we often took the same walk at the same hour. I said nothing about the dog, figuring that the subject would come up on its own.

"Oh, yes," he said. "'I'm eighty-six years old, and I'm downtown at seven o'clock every morning. I'm retired, but I don't stay still. 1 work as a porter for the law firm of Bouhan, Williams and Levy." Mr. Glover's voice had a bounce to it. He pronounced the name of the law firm as if an exclamation mark followed each of the partners' names.

"I'm a porter, but everybody knows me as a singer," he said as we started to cross the street. "I learned to sing in church when I was twelve. I pumped the organ for a quarter while one iady played and another lady sang. I didn't know nothing about no German, French, or Italian, but by me hearing the lady sing so much, I learned to say the words whether I knew what they was or not. One Sunday morning, jgj the ladv didn't sing, so I sang instead. And I sang in Italian, I sang 'Hallelujah.'"

"How did it go?" I asked him.

Mr. Glover stopped and faced me. He opened his mouth wide and drew a deep breath. From the back of his throat came a high, croaking sound, "Aaaaa lay loooo-yah! A-layyyy-loo yah!" He had abandoned his tenor and was singing in a wavering falsetto. Forever m his mind. apparently, "Hallelujah" would be a soprano piece as sung by the lady in church so many years before. "Allay-loo-yah, a-lay-loo yah, a-lay-loo yah, a-lay-loo yah, a-lay-loo-yah, a-lay-loo-yah!" Mr. Glover stopped for a breath. "— And then the lady always finished by saying, 'AAAAAAAhhh lay looooooo yah!'

"So that was your debut," I said.

"That's right! That's how I started. That lady learned me to sing in German, French, and Italian! Oh, yes! And I've been musical director of the First African Baptist Church since 1916. I directed a chorus of five hundred voices for Franklin D. Roosevelt when he visited Savannah on November 18, 1933. I remember the date, because that was the very day my daughter was born. I named her Eleanor Roosevelt Glover. I can remember the song we sang too: 'Come By Here.' The doctor sent word up to me. 'Tell Glover he can sing "Gome By Here" for the president all he damn pleases, but I just come by his house and left a baby

girl and I want him to come by mv office and pay me fifteen dollars.'"

When we parted at the corner of Oglethorpe Avenue, I
realized I was still in the dark about the imaginary dog,
Patrick. A week or so later, when I next fell in step with
Mr. Glover, I made a mental note to bring the subject
around to it. But Mr. Glover had other things to talk
about first.

"You know about psychology," he said. "You learn that in
school. You learn *people*-ology on the Pullman. I was a porter
for the Pullman during the war. You had to keep the passen-
gers well satisfied for 'em to tip you fifty cents or a dollar.
You say, 'Wait a minute, sir. You going up to the club car?
Your tie is crooked.' Now, his tie is really straight as an
arrow, but you pull it crooked and then you pull it straight
again, and he likes it. That's people-ology!

"Keep a whisk broom in your pocket, and brush him off!
He don't need no brushing off, but he don't know it! Brush
hun off anyhow, and straighten his collar. Pull it crooked and
straighten it again. Miss Mamie don't need a box for her hat,
but you be sure and put her hat in a box! If you sit and don't
do nothin', you won't get nothin'!

"Another thing I learned: Don't ever ask a man, 'How is
Mrs Brown?' You ask him, 'How is Miss Julia? *Tell her I ask
about her.*' I never did ask Mr. Bouhan about Mrs. Bouhan. I
ask him, 'How is Miss Helen? *Tell Miss Helen I ask about
her.*' He liked it and she liked it. Mr. Bouhan gave me his
old clothes and shoes. Miss Helen gave me records from her
collection, all kinds of records. I got records I don't even

know I got. I even got records of that great opera singer... Henry Coca-ruso!

"I keep busy," Mr. Glover said. "I don't sit down and hold my hand. I got five hundred dollars of life insurance, and it's all paid up. I paid twenty-five cents a week for seventy years! And last week the Metropolitan Life Insurance Company sent me a check for one thousand dollars!"

Mr. Glover's eyes were sparkling. "No, sir, I don't sit down and hold my hand."

"Glover!" came a booming voice from behind us. A tall white-haired man in a gray suit approached. "Still walking the dog?"

"Why, yes, sir, yes I am," Mr. Glover did his little bow and tipped his hat and gestured to the invisible dog behind him. "I'm still walking Patrick."

"Glad to hear it. Glover, Keep it np! Tike care now." With that, the man walked away.

"How long have you been walking Patrick?" I asked.

Mr. Glover straightened up. "Oh, for a long time. Patrick was Mr. Bouhan's dog. Mr. Bouhan used to give him Chivas Regal scotch liquor to drink. I walked the dog, and I was the dog's bartender too. Mr. Bouhan said that after he died I was to be paid ten dollars a week to take care of Patrick. He put that in his will. I had to walk him and buy his scotch liquor. When Patrick died, I went to see Judge Lawrence. The judge was Mr. Bouhan's executor. I said, 'Judge, you can stop paying me the ten dollars now, because Patrick is dead.' And Judge Lawrence said, 'What do you mean Patrick is dead? How could he be? I see him right there! Right there on the carpet.' I looked behind me, and I didn't see no dog. But then I thought a minute and I said, 'Oh! I think I see him too, Judge!' And the judge said, 'Good. So you iust keep walking him and we'll keep paying you.' The dog is dead twenty years now, but I still walk him. I walk up and down Bull Street and look over my shoulder and say, 'Gome on, Patrick!'"

MEMORIES

John Galsworthy

WE SET OUT TO MEET HIM at Waterloo Station on a dull
day of February — I, who had owned his impetuous mother,
knowing a little what to expect, while to my companion he
would be all original. We stood there waiting (for the
Salisbury train was late), and wondering with a warm, half-
fearful eagerness what sort of new thread Life was going to
twine into our skein. I think our chief dread was that he
might have light eyes — those yellow Chinese eyes of the
common, parti-colored spaniel. And each new minute of the
train's tardiness increased our anxious compassion: His first
journey; his first separation from his mother; this black two-
months' baby! Then the train ran in, and we hastened to
look for him. "Have you a dog for us?"

"A dog! Not in this van. Ask the rear-guard."

"Have you a dog for us?"

"That's right. From Salisbury. Here's your wild beast, sir!"

From behind a wooden crate we saw a long black muzzled nose poking round at us, and heard a faint hoarse whimpering.

I remember my first thought:

"Isn't his nose too long?"

But to my companion's heart it went at once, because it was swollen from crying and being pressed against things that he could not see through. We took him out, soft, wobbly, tearful; set him down on his four as yet not quite simultaneous legs, and regarded him. Or, rather, my companion did, having her head on one side, and a quavering smile; and I regarded her, knowing that I should thereby get a truer impression of him.

He wandered a little round our legs, neither wagging his tail nor licking at our hands; then he looked up, and my companion said: "He's an angel!"

I was not so certain. He seemed hammer-headed, with no eyes at all, and little connection between his head, his body, and his legs. His ears were very long, as long as his poor nose; and gleaming down in the blackness of him I could see the same white star that disgraced his mother's chest.

Picking him up, we carried him to a four-wheeled cab, and took his muzzle off. His little dark-brown eyes were resolutely fixed on distance, and by his refusal to even smell the biscuits we had brought to make him happy, we knew that the human being had not yet come into a life that had contained so far only a mother, a wood-shed, and four other soft, wobbly, black, hammer-headed angels, smelling of themselves, and warmth, and wood shavings. It was pleasant to feel that to us he would surrender an untouched love, that is, if he would surrender anything. Suppose he did not take to us!

And just then something must have stirred in him, for he turned up his swollen nose and stared at my companion, and a little later rubbed the dry pinkness of his tongue against my thumb. In that look, and that unconscious restless lick, he was trying hard to leave unhappiness behind, trying hard to feel that these new creatures with stroking paws and queer scents were his mother; yet all the time he knew, I am sure, that they were something bigger, more permanently, desperately, his. The first sense of being owned, perhaps (who knows) of owning, had stirred in him. He would never again be quite the same unconscious creature.

A little way from the end of our journey we got out and dismissed the cab. He could not too soon know the scents and pavements of this London where the chief of his life must pass. I can see now his first bumble down that wide, backwater of a street, how continually and suddenly he sat down to make sure of his own legs, how continually he lost our heels. He showed us then in full perfection what was afterwards to be an inconvenient — if endearing — characteristic: At any call or whistle he would look in precisely the opposite direction. How many times all through his life have I not seen him, at my whistle, start violently and turn his tail to me, then, with nose thrown searchingly from side to side, begin to canter toward the horizon!

In that first walk, we met, fortunately, but one vehicle, a brewer's dray; he chose that moment to attend to the more serious affairs of life, sitting quietly before the horses' feet and requiring to be moved by hand. From the beginning he had his dignity, and was extremely difficult to lift, owing to the length of his middle distance.

What strange feelings must have stirred in his little white soul when he first smelled carpet! But it was all so strange to him that day — I doubt if he felt more than I did when I first travelled to my private school, reading "Tales of a Grandfather," and plied with tracts and sherry by my father's man of business.

That night, indeed, for several nights, he slept with me, keeping me too warm down my back, and waking me now and then with quaint sleepy whimperings. Indeed, all through his life he flew a good deal in his sleep, fighting dogs and seeing ghosts, running after rabbits and thrown sticks; and to the last one never quite knew whether or not to rouse him when his four black feet began to jerk and quiver. His dreams were like our dreams, both good and bad; happy sometimes, sometimes tragic to weeping point.

He ceased to sleep with me the day we discovered that he was a perfect little colony, whose settlers were of an active species which I have never seen again. After that he had many beds, for circumstance ordained that his life should be nomadic, and it is to this I trace that philosophic indifference to place or property, which marked him out from most of his own kind. He learned early that for a black dog with long silky ears, a feathered tail, and head of great dignity, there was no home whatsoever, away from those creatures with special scents, who took liberties with his name, and alone of all created things were privileged to smack him with a slipper. He would sleep anywhere, so long as it was in their room, or so close outside it as to make no matter, for it was with him a principle that what he did not smell did not exist. I would I could hear again those long rubber-lipped snufflings of recognition underneath the door, with which each morning he would regale and reassure a spirit that grew with age more and more nervous and delicate about this matter of propinquity! For he was a dog of fixed ideas, things stamped on his mind were indelible; as, for example, his duty toward cats, for whom he had really a perverse affection, which had led to that first disastrous moment of his life, when he was brought up, poor bewildered puppy, from a brief excursion to the kitchen, with one eye closed and his cheek torn! He bore to his grave that jagged scratch across the eye. It was in dread of a repetition of this tragedy that he was instructed at the word "Cats" to rush forward with a special "tow-row-row-ing," which he never used toward any other form of creature. To the end he cherished a hope that he would reach the cat, but never did; and if he had, we knew he would only have stood and wagged his tail; but I well remember once, when he returned, important, from some such sally, how dreadfully my companion startled a cat-loving friend by murmuring in her most honeyed voice: "Well, my darling, have you been killing pussies in the garden?"

His eye and nose were impeccable in their sense of form; indeed, he was very English in that matter: People must be just so; things smell properly; and affairs go on in the one right way. He could tolerate neither creatures in ragged clothes, nor children on their hands and knees, nor postmen, because, with their bags, they swelled-up on one side, and carried lanterns on their stomachs. He would never let the harmless creatures pass without religious barks. Naturally a believer in authority and routine, and distrusting spiritual adventure, he yet had curious fads that seemed to have nested in him, quite outside of all principle. He would, for instance, follow neither carriages nor horses, and if we tried to make him, at once left for home, where he would sit with nose raised to Heaven, emitting through it a most lugubrious, shrill noise. Then again, one must not place a stick, a slipper, a glove, or anything with which he could play, upon one's head — since such an action reduced him at once to frenzy. For so conservative a dog, his environment was sadly anarchistic. He never complained in words of our shifting habits, but curled his head round over his left paw and pressed his chin very hard against the ground whenever he smelled packing. What necessity — he seemed continually to be saying — what real necessity is there for change of any kind whatever? Here we were all together, and one day was like another, so that I knew where I was — and now you only know what will happen next; and I — I can't tell you whether I shall be with you when it happens! What strange, grieving minutes a dog passes at such times in the underground of his subconsciousness, refusing realisation, yet all the time only too well divining. Some careless word, some unmuted compassion in voice, the stealthy wrapping of a pair of boots, the unaccustomed shutting of a door that ought to be open, the removal from a down-stair room of an object always there — one tiny thing, and he knows for certain that he is not going too. He fights against the knowledge just as we do against what we cannot bear; he gives up hope, but not effort, protesting in the only way he knows of, and now and then heaving a great sigh. Those sighs of a dog! They go to the heart so much more deeply than the sighs of our own kind, because they are utterly unintended, regardless of effect, emerging from one who, heaving them, knows not that they have escaped him!

The words: "Yes—going too!" spoken in a certain tone, would call up in his eyes a still-questioning half-happiness, and from his tail a quiet flutter, but did not quite serve to put to rest either his doubt or his feeling that it was all unnecessary — until the cab arrived. Then he would pour himself out of door or window, and be found in the bottom of the vehicle, looking severely away from an admiring cabman. Once settled on our feet he travelled with philosophy, but no digestion.

I think no dog was ever more indifferent to an outside world of human creatures; yet few dogs have made more conquests — especially among strange women, through whom, however, he had a habit of looking — very discouraging. He had, natheless, one or two particular friends, and a few persons whom he knew he had seen before, but, broadly speaking, there were in his world of men, only his mistress, and — the almighty.

Each August, till he was six, he was sent for health, and the assuagement of his hereditary instincts, up to a Scotch shooting, where he carried many birds in a very tender manner. Once he was compelled by Fate to remain there nearly a year; and we went up ourselves to fetch him home. Down the long avenue toward the keeper's cottage we walked. It was high autumn; there had been frost already, for the ground was fine with red and yellow leaves; and presently we saw himself coming, professionally questing among those leaves, and preceding his dear keeper with the businesslike self-containment of a sportsman; not too fat, glossy as a raven's wing, swinging his ears and sporran like a little Highlander. We approached him silently. Suddenly his nose went up from its imagined trail, and he came rushing at our legs. From him, as a garment drops from a man, dropped all his strange soberness; he became in a single instant one fluttering eagerness. He leaped from life to life in one bound, without hesitation, without regret. Not one sigh, not one look back, not the faintest token of gratitude or regret at leaving those good people who had tended him for a whole year, buttered oat-cake for him, allowed him to choose each night exactly where he would sleep. No, he just marched out beside us, as close as ever he could get, drawing us on in spirit, and not even attending to the scents, until the lodge gates were passed.

It was strictly in accordance with the perversity of things, and something in the nature of calamity that he had not been ours one year, when there came over me a dreadful but over-mastering aversion from killing those birds and creatures of which he was so fond as soon as they were dead. And so I never knew him as a sportsman; for during that first year he was only an unbroken puppy, tied to my waist for fear of accidents, and carefully pulling me off every shot. They tell me he developed a lovely nose and perfect mouth, large enough to hold gingerly the biggest hare. I well believe it, remembering the qualities of his mother, whose character, however, in stability he far surpassed. But as he grew every year more devoted to dead grouse and birds and rabbits, I liked them more and more alive; it was the only real breach between us, and we kept it out of sight. Ah! well; it is consoling to reflect that I should infallibly have ruined his sporting qualities, lacking that peculiar habit of meaning what one says, so necessary to keep dogs virtuous. But surely to have had him with me, quivering and alert, with his solemn, eager face, would have given a new joy to those crisp mornings when the hope of wings coming to the gun makes poignant in the sportsman, as nothing else will, an almost sensual love of Nature, a fierce delight in the soft glow of leaves, in the white birch stems and tracery of sparse twigs against blue sky, in the scents of sap and grass and gum and heather flowers; stivers the hair of him with keenness for interpreting each sound, and fills the very fern or moss he kneels on, the very trunk he leans against, with strange vibration.

Slowly Fate prepares for each of us the religion that lies coiled in our most secret nerves; with such we cannot trifle, we do not even try! But how shall a man grudge any one sensations he has so keenly felt? Let such as have never known those curious delights uphold the hand of horror — for me there can be no such luxury. If I could, I would still perhaps be knowing them; but when once the joy of life in those winged and furry things has knocked at the very portals of one's spirit, the thought that by pressing a little iron twig one will rive that joy out of their vitals is too hard to bear. Call it aestheticism, squeamishness, namby-pamby sentimentalism, what you will — it is stronger than oneself!

Yes, after one had once watched with an eye that did not merely see, the thirsty gaping of a slowly dying bird, or a rabbit dragging a broken leg to a hole where he would lie for hours thinking of the fern to which he should never more come forth — after that, there was always the following little matter of arithmetic: Given, that all those who had been shooting were "good-fair" shots — which, Heaven knew, they never were — they yet missed one at least in four, and did not miss it very much; so that if seventy-five things were slain, there were also twenty-five that had been fired at, and, of those twenty-five, twelve and a half had "gotten it" somewhere in their bodies, and would "likely" die at their great leisure.

This was the sum that brought about the only cleavage in our lives; and so, as he grew older, and trying to part from each other we no longer could, he ceased going to Scotland. But after that I often felt, and especially when we heard guns, how the best and most secret instincts of him were being stifled. But what was to be done? In that which was left of a clay pigeon he would take not the faintest interest — the scent of it was paltry. Yet always, even in his most cosseted and idle days, he managed to preserve the grave preoccupation of one professionally concerned with retrieving things that smell; and consoled himself with pastimes such as cricket, which he played in a manner highly specialised, following the ball up the moment it left the bowler's hand, and sometimes retrieving it before it reached the batsman. When remonstrated with, he would consider a little, hanging out a pink tongue and looking rather too eagerly at the ball, then canter slowly out to a sort of forward short leg. Why he always chose that particular position it is difficult to say; possibly he could lurk there better than anywhere else, the batsman's eye not being on him, and the bowler's not too much. As a fieldsman he was perfect, but for an occasional belief that he was not merely short leg, but slip, point, mid-off, and wicket-keep; and perhaps a tendency to make the ball a little "jubey." But he worked tremendously, watching every movement; for he knew the game thoroughly, and seldom delayed it more than three minutes when he secured the ball. And if that ball were really lost, then indeed he took over the proceedings with an intensity and quiet vigor that destroyed many shrubs, and the solemn satisfaction which comes from being in the very centre of the stage.

But his most passionate delight was swimming in anything except the sea, for which, with its unpleasant noise and habit of tasting salt, he had little affection. I see him now, cleaving the Serpentine, with his air of "the world well lost," striving to reach my stick before it had touched water. Being only a large spaniel, too small for mere heroism, he saved no lives in the water but his own — and that, on one occasion, before our very eyes, from a dark trout stream, which was trying to wash him down into a black hole among the boulders.

The call of the wild — Spring running — whatever it is

— that besets men and dogs, seldom attained full mastery over him; but one could often see it struggling against his devotion to the scent of us, and, watching that dumb contest, I have time and again wondered how far this civilisation of ours was justifiably imposed on him; how far the love for us that we had so carefully implanted could ever replace in him the satisfaction of his primitive wild yearnings. He was like a man, naturally polygamous, married to one loved woman.

It was surely not for nothing that Rover is dog's most common name, and would be ours, but for our too tenacious fear of losing something, to admit, even to ourselves, that we are hankering. There was a man who said: Strange that two such queerly opposite qualities as courage and hypocrisy are the leading characteristics of the Anglo-Saxon! But is not hypocrisy just a product of tenacity, which is again the lower part of courage? Is not hypocrisy but an active sense of property in one's good name, the clutching close of respectability at any price, the feeling that one must not part, even at the cost of truth, with what he has sweated so to gain? And so we Anglo-Saxons will not answer to the name of Rover, and treat our dogs so that they, too, hardly know their natures.

The history of his one wandering, for which no respectable reason can be assigned, will never, of course, be known. It was in London, of an October evening, when we were told he had slipped out and was not anywhere. Then began those four distressful hours of searching for that black needle in that blacker bundle of hay. Hours of real dismay and suffering — for it is suffering, indeed, to feel a loved thing swallowed up in that hopeless maze of London streets. Stolen or run over? Which was worst? The neighboring police stations visited, the Dog's Home notified, an order for five hundred "Lost Dog" bills placed in the printer's hands, the streets patrolled! And then, in a lull snatched for food, and still endeavoring to preserve some aspect of assurance, we heard the bark which meant: "Here is a door I cannot open!" We hurried forth, and there he was on the top doorstep — busy, unashamed, giving no explanations, asking for his supper; and very shortly after him came his five hundred "Lost Dog" bills. Long I sat looking at him that night after my companion had gone up, thinking of the evening, some years before, when there followed us that shadow of a spaniel who had been lost for eleven days. And my heart turned over within me. But he! He was asleep, for he knew not remorse.

Ah! and there was that other time, when it was reported to me, returning home at night, that he had gone out to find me; and I went forth again, disturbed, and whistling his special call to the empty fields. Suddenly out of the darkness I heard a rushing, and he came furiously dashing against my heels for he alone knew where he had been lurking and saying to himself: I will not go in till he comes! I could not scold, there was something too lyrical in the return of that live, lonely, rushing piece of blackness through the blacker night. After all, the vagary was but a variation in his practice when one was away at bed-time, of passionately scratching up his bed in protest, till it resembled nothing; for, in spite of his long and solemn face and the silki-ness of his ears, there was much in him yet of the cave bear —he dug graves on the smallest provocations, in which he never buried anything. He was not a "clever" dog; and guiltless of all tricks. Nor was he ever "shown." We did not even dream of subjecting him to this indignity. Was our dog a clown, a hobby, a fad, a fashion, a feather in our caps—that we should subject him to periodic pennings in stuffy halls, that we should harry his faithful soul with such tomfoolery? He never even heard us talk about his lineage, deplore the length of his nose, or call him "clever-looking." We should have been ashamed to let him smell about us the tar-brush of a sense of property, to let him think we looked on him as an asset to earn us pelf or glory. We wished that there should be between us the spirit that was between the sheep-dog and that farmer, who, when asked his dog's age, touched the old creature's head, and answered thus: "Teresa" (his daughter) "was born in November, and this one in August." That sheep-dog had seen eighteen years when the great white day came for him, and his spirit passed away up, to cling with the wood-smoke round the dark rafters of the kitchen where he had lain so vast a time beside his master's boots. No, no! If a man does not soon pass beyond the thought: "By what shall this dog profit me?" into the large state of simple gladness to be with dog, he shall never know the very essence of that companionship which depends not on the points of dog, but on some strange and subtle mingling of mute spirits. For it is by muteness that a dog becomes for one so utterly beyond value; with him one is at peace, where words play no torturing tricks. When he just sits, loving, and knows that he is being loved, those are the moments that I think are precious to a dog; when, with his adoring soul coming through his eyes, he feels that you are really thinking of him. But he is touchingly tolerant of one's other occupations. The subject of these memories always knew when one was too absorbed in work to be so close to him as he thought proper; yet he never tried to hinder or distract, or asked for attention. It dinged his mood, of course, so that the red under his eyes and the folds of his crumply cheeks — which seemed to speak of a touch of bloodhound introduced a long way back into his breeding — grew deeper and more manifest. If he could have spoken at such times, he would have said: "I have been a long time alone, and I cannot always be asleep; but you know best, and I must not criticise."

He did not at all mind one's being absorbed in other humans: he seemed to enjoy the sounds of conversation lifting round him, and to know when they were sensible. He could not, for instance, stand actors or actresses giving readings of their parts, perceiving at once that the same had no connection with the minds and real feelings of the speakers; and, having wandered a little to show his disapproval, he would go to the door and stare at it till it opened and let him out. Once or twice, it is true, when an actor of large voice was declaiming an emotional passage, he so far relented as to go up to him and pant in his face. Music, too, made him restless, inclined to sigh, and to ask questions. Sometimes, at its first sound, he would cross to the window and remain there looking for Her. At others, he would simply go and lie on the loud pedal, and we never could tell whether it was from sentiment, or because he thought that in this way he heard less. At one special Nocturne of Chopin's he always whimpered. He *was*, indeed, of rather Polish temperament — very gay when he was gay, dark and brooding when he was not.

On the whole, perhaps his life was uneventful for so far-travelling a dog, though it held its moments of eccentricity, as when he leaped through the window of a four-wheeler into Kensington, or sat on a Dartmoor adder. But that was fortunately of a Sunday afternoon — when adder and all were torpid, so nothing happened, till a friend, who was following, lifted him off the creature with his large boot.

If only one could have known more of his private life — more of his relations with his own kind! I fancy he was always rather a dark dog to them, having so many thoughts about us that he could not share with any one, and being naturally fastidious, except with ladies, for whom he had a chivalrous and catholic taste, so that they often turned and snapped at him. He had, however, but one lasting love affair, for a liver-colored lass of our village, not quite of his own caste, but a wholesome if somewhat elderly girl, with loving and sphinx-like eyes. Their children, alas, were not for this world, and soon departed.

Nor was he a fighting dog; but once attacked, he lacked a sense of values, being unable to distinguish between dogs that he could beat and dogs with whom he had "no earthly." It was, in fact, as well to interfere at once, especially in the matter of retrievers, for he never forgot having in his youth been attacked by a retriever from behind. No, he never forgot, and never forgave, an enemy. Only a month before that day of which I cannot speak, being very old and ill, he engaged an Irish terrier on whose impudence he had long had his eye, and routed him. And how a battle cheered his spirit! He was certainly no Christian; but, allowing for essential dog, he was very much a gentleman. And I do think that most of us who live on this earth these days would rather leave it with that label on us than the other. For to be a Christian, as Tolstoy understood the word — and no one else in our time has had logic and love of truth enough to give it coherent meaning — is (to be quite sincere) not suited to men of Western blood. Whereas — to be a gentleman! It is a far cry, but perhaps it can be done. In him, at all events, there was no pettiness, no meanness, and no cruelty, and though he fell below his ideal at times, this never altered the true look of his eyes, nor the simple loyalty in his soul.

But what a crowd of memories come back, bringing with them the perfume of fallen days! What delights and glamour, what long hours of effort, discouragements, and secret fears did he not watch over—our black familiar; and with the sight and scent and touch of him, deepen or assuage! How many thousand walks did we not go together, so that we still turn to see if he is following at his padding gait, attentive to the invisible trails. Not the least hard thing to bear when they go from us, these quiet friends, is that they carry away with them so many years of our own lives. Yet, if they find warmth therein, who would grudge them those years that they have so guarded? Nothing else of us can they take to lie upon with outstretched paws and chin pressed to the ground; and, whatever they take, be sure they have deserved.

Do they know, as we do, that their time must come? Yes, they know, at rare moments. No other way can I interpret those pauses of his latter life, when, propped on his forefeet, he would sit for long minutes quite motionless — his head drooped, utterly withdrawn; then turn those eyes of his and look at me. That look said more plainly than all words could: "Yes, I know that I must go!" If *we* have spirits that persist — *they* have. If *we* know, after our departure, who we were — *they* do. No one, I think, who really longs for truth, can ever glibly say which it will be for dog and man — persistence or extinction of our consciousness. There is but one thing certain — the childishness of fretting over that eternal question. Whichever it be, it must be right, the only possible thing. He felt that too, I know; but then, like his master, he was what is called a pessimist.

My companion tells me that, since he left us, he has once come back. It was Old Year's Night, and she was sad, when he came to her in visible shape of his black body, passing round the dining-table from the window-end, to his proper place beneath the table, at her feet. She saw him quite clearly; she heard the padding tap-tap of his paws and very toe-nails; she felt his warmth brushing hard against the front of her skirt. She thought then that he would settle down upon her feet, but something disturbed him, and he stood pausing, pressed against her, then moved out toward where I generally sit, but was not sitting that night. She saw him stand there, as if considering; then at some sound or laugh,

206

TO ABSENT FRIENDS

she became self-conscious, and slowly, very slowly, he was no longer there. Had he some message, some counsel to give, something he would say, that last night of the last year of all those he had watched over us? Will he come back again?

No stone stands over where he lies. It is on our hearts that his life is engraved.

So Long, Pal

Burton Spiller

WHEN I FIRST MET YOU the shooting season had ended, and the leaden New England skies seemed doubly cheerless because I had just lost your predecessor. Into that somber period of my life you came like a sun-kissed morning. I recall the day perfectly.

I was sitting morosely by the fire, pondering why a malicious fate so often casts a somber shadow over our lives. Then your owner drove into the yard with you and five of your brothers and sisters. I remember that when we opened the crates and you all came tumbling out pandemonium immediately ensued. Such leapings and twistings and turnings! Such mad dashings across the field! Such a turmoil of yelpings which filled the air with their clamor, and dwarfed to nothing the exuberant cries of skaters rioting on the river, yet strangely it was a soothing sound to me. The leaden skies seemed to lighten, and all at once there was warmth and friendliness in the crisp December air.

I wish I might tell you that I knew from the first moment that you were going to be my dog, but that would not be strictly true. There were too many of your kind, a liver-and-white kaleidoscope that would not be still a moment. But gradually I became aware that there was one bit of atomic energy that frequently separated itself from its fellows and returned to its master for a friendly word. That was you, old boy I knew you then. You were a one-man dog, and you were going to be mine.

I have never regretted my decision, and I like to think that in all the years we were together you never had occasion to regret it either. You see, I had formed an opinion concerning the ideal relationship between a dog and its master which was somewhat at variance with my youthful conception of the status. I had learned that a dog was as much an individual as was a man, and I had come to believe that as long as it was compatible with good bird work, a dog should be encouraged to express his individuality If he had his own ideas concerning the best way to handle a running pheasant or ruffed grouse, it might be better for me to modify my views slightly, instead of trying to mold the dog to my inflexible will.

I had vowed, too, that by every artifice at my command I would trv to make my dog think that I was the most wonderful person in the world. He should be taught to mind promptly both signal and spoken commands, but there would be no hint of harshness in the teaching. Firmness, yes, but a gentle firmness that would leave no taint of unpleasantness for him to ponder over when he was alone.

And so I opened my home to you. You had your tufted pad in the kitchen. You owned one end of the davenport in the living room, and the upholstered chair in the den was yours by divine right. From the other rooms, and from the chambers, you were barred, but after you had worked your way into the heart of the gracious lady of the manor, I could sometimes hear the stealthy pad of your feet upon the stairs as you inched your way upward and into her room to wriggle an ecstatic good-morning welcome.

I remember how your soft brown eyes finally won for you, and how after a time you would remain there until you heard me open a door which led outside, when you would come tearing down, leaving a devastation of scattered rugs behind you, and vault in a long, arching curve out into your great and beautiful world.

Then you changed from a gangling six-months pup, whose feet and one end or the other were always a size too large, into a sleek and muscular creature whose every lithe movement was so graceful that it would cause a constriction in my throat just to watch you. We were compatible, you and I, for my system worked in your training. Five minutes time was all that was needed to teach you to hold as steady as a rock on your plate of food, and you won your sheep-skin in retrieving after six easy lessons.

From the first day I took you afield you hunted with a joyous lightness that was my conception of perfection. Your nose spurned the earth as did your feet. You were airborne from the moment we entered a cover until we emerged from it, flitting here and there before me as smoothly as a swallow, while with your head uplifted you quested the air for game scent, yet slowing abruptly and advancing with tiptoeing caution whenever your unerring nose caught the first elusive fragment of it.

How wonderful they were, those first magic days that we spent together in the woods. The surrounding hills were no more immovable than you when you stretched out in one of your glorious points. No command of mine could move you as long as a ruffed grouse crouched in a thicket before you, as you proved to me on one of the very first days we hunted together.

You had disappeared from my sight in fairly thick cover, and after waiting a decent interval I drifted ahead with hope that I would find you on point, but you were not there. With hurrying strides I went the length of the cover, and emerged into a more open one where only a few scattered pines grew. You were young and ambitious, and I thought the open country had challenged you to explore it; so I covered that, too. fearful lest I had lost you, and wondering if you had picked up enough woods lore to enable you to pick up my trail and follow it.

I was blowing my whistle then, shrilly and at frequent intervals and, still blowing it, I returned to that part of the cover where I had last seen you. There was one small open- ing in that tangle of birch and alders and by mere chance I blundered into one end of it. There you were at the other end, locked in a fiery point that a half hour of waiting had not quenched by a single degree.

There was always something about your points which

made me a better man with a gun. You were so infallibly right when you slid into that animated but immobile pose, that it sometimes lifted me to supreme heights. So it was on that occasion. The grouse rose at a thirty-yard range and had less than ten more to go to reach screening cover, yet I killed it without any sensation of hurrying and I had several feet to spare.

In the woods you were a dog who could be depended upon to the last minute of the day but at home you were sometimes unpredictable. I recall the occasion of Ray Holland's first visit with us. No one had told you that Ray was editor-in-chief of Field & Stream, and that he was paving for much of your bread and butter, or you might have acted differently.

Everything was normal for a time, and then that awkward moment arrived when conversation suddenly lagged. I was groping desperately for a topic, like a circus elephant wondering where the next peanut is coming from, when I thought of you.

You had a queer little trick of curling your right forefoot inward and lowering your head a trifle, and I had elaborated upon it until at a secret signal from me you would make a deep and exquisitely polite bow. We had rehearsed it until we had it perfected, and now it seemed like a life-saver. I went out and got you, put you smartly at heel, and we came in snappily like the well-trained pair we were.

In the doorway I paused abruptly, said, "Pal, this is Ray Holland," and took one step aside, which was the cue to do your stuff. In that sudden and awful silence, you looked at him calmly up and down, from his slightly thinning hair to the tips of his well-polished shoes — and yawned prodigiously Then, with an air of melancholy that only Hamlet could have equalled, you turned and went back to the obscurity from which I had summoned you, and curled up on your mat to resume your interrupted slumber.

There was another occasion when we entertained equally distinguished guests at dinner. Everything was painfully formal and polite, and so far as real genial warmth was concerned we might as well have been dining in an igloo. Then my ears detected a sound which filled me with startled apprehension. It was the sound of your teeth clamping down on the metal rim of your food pan. You came bounding in, your nails screeched as they brought you to a skidding halt beside the table, you banged the dish down on the floor, took a backward step and looked expectantly up at us as though to say "Hey you guys! Don't I rate a plate of food from a setup like this?"

You got the food, as you undoubtedly knew you would, and it was the Most Distinguished Guest who passed the collection plate, but even before you had finished bolting the last fragment a miracle had taken place. All our stiff formality had vanished, and we were really enjoying a friendship which has been a lasting one.

I remember, too, the day when you gave me the coldest bath I have ever experienced. We were hunting woodcock in the Nighthawk Cover, a mile-long strip of alder tangle through which ran a brawling, turbulent brook. It was late in the season. The ground had frozen the previous night, and even now with the sun two hours high there was a rim of ice around the edges of each upthrust boulder in the brook.

We had hunted the length of the cover, and now I was searching for a place where I could cross the stream. Ordinarily there were numerous spots where one could step from stone to stone and win the opposite bank with feet still dry; but on this day the water was far above its normal level and the stepping-stones were few and mighty far between.

I found a place which showed possibilities. It was not entirely to my liking, for it required five jumps, and the third one — in the center of the stream — was at least three feet out of line. The trick would have to be accomplished at high speed if it were accomplished at all, and I had a growing conviction that to pivot on that rounded boulder in midstream, and then spring off at a tangent for the remaining two, would require perfect co-ordination of both mind and muscle.

Standing on the bank, and deliberating the problem of which foot should touch which stone, I became so engrossed that I forgot another and equally important factor. The most rigid schooling I had given you consisted of crossing a street in the midst of heavy traffic. I would put you at heel and wait for a favorable opportunity When it presented itself. I would tug mightily on your leash and we would shoot across the street in nothing flat. You learned to do it perfectly after a time, adjusting your pace to mine so accurately that we were never separated by more than a few inches. That was the factor I should have remembered.

Clutching the gun in one hand and my hat in the other, I leaped for the first boulder, and from the tail of my eye I

To Absent Friends

saw your agile form take flight at the same moment. The situation. I could readily see, was about to become complicated unless I was man enough to beat you to the other shore. No boulder had room for more than one foot at any time, and to attempt to place five on it simultaneously could only result in disaster.

I beat you to the first one by inches, but we struck the second one together. Somehow I managed to secure enough leverage to make that twisting, third leap, and I made it with a sure foreknowledge of what was about to happen. It was necessary for me to achieve quite a bit of altitude in order to span the distance, but your wiry muscles gave you a natter trajector.

You were fairly on the boulder and contracting your sinews for another leap when I came down upon you. You emitted one startled yelp, which was dwarfed to insignificance by my resounding splash, and then the icy waters closed over us. You were the first ashore, and with a vigorous shake you were ready to go again, but I had to strip off the last dripping thread and wring the water from it. Ah, me! We were thirty miles from home, and we were hunting woodcock. We took our limit that day with a brace of grouse thrown in for good measure, and we went home after night had fallen, dry and warm and inordinately happy.

One of the most satisfying things about the years we hunted together was the fact that I never knew you to fail to find a crippled bird. I believe a dog requires a far keener nose to locate dead or crippled game than he does to find an uninjured one, but whether or not this is true you had the thing required. You surprised me many times by bringing in a bird I believed I had missed cleanly.

There was a day when we were hunting woodcock along the shores of Lake Winnipesaukee. It was exceptionally open cover, and there was absolutely no excuse for missing any bird that got up within range; but I did it on a perfect straightaway It was so entirely unexpected that I was disconcerted for a moment, and instead of redeeming myself with the second barrel I watched the bird fly a hundred yards and then flutter down into another sparse clump of alders.

You always gave me a puzzled look whenever I missed a bird, and on that occasion I could plainly read the question in your eyes. "What's the matter, boss?" they asked. "Slipping?"

I admitted it and told you to go find that woodcock. "Show him to me once more and I'll prove to you whether I'm slipping or not," I said, and you went down the cover and locked up on another of your spectacular points.

I kicked the bird out, killed it cleanly and sent you in to get it. Somehow you were never really enthusiastic about bringing in a woodcock. Knock down a grouse for you, and you would rush in and grab it, then come bounding back with a million-dollar light in your eves, but the little russet fellows always left you emotionally cold. Your attitude seemed to say. "It's swell sport hunting them, boss. I like to point them and I like to see you bowl them over, but what the heck do you care for them after they're dead?"

So you went dutifully in after the bird and started out

with it. Then you hesitated, slowed to a walk, stopped, dropped the bird and began working the cover at your right.

I said to you, "Haven't you heard that a bird in the hand is worth two in the bush? Cut the fooling around, get down to business and bring me that bird."

You might have been deaf for all the attention you gave me. Methodically you quartered the thicket, swung sharply left, picked up a woodcock and came plodding out with it.

"I killed the first bird after all," I thought, but carefully refrained from voicing more than a polite thank you when you dropped it in my hand, for I was curious to learn if your reasoning powers were equal to the occasion.

If there was even a suspicion of doubt in my mind, I'm sorry for it, for of your own accord you went back and found the bird you had dropped, then came bounding back, passed it up to me, and your look seemed to say "How's that, huh? Don't you think I'm a pretty good sort of a guy to have around?"

I always thought your were. I miss you. Only yesterday I found myself pausing with my hand on the open door as I waited for the familiar thud of your feet as you landed beside me. You had an habitual disregard for those first three steps, and always went from the bottom to the top in one effortless leap. Undoubtedly I shall wait thus for you many more times. I wish it were possible for you to know that.

You left an impressive volume of memories for me to cherish, but of them all I think the last time we hunted together will remain clear the longest. For weeks I had known the disquieting feeling that you would not be with me much longer, but when the veterinarian told me so it came as a distinct shock. There had always been the hope that a miracle might happen, but now I could no longer hope. Yours was a tremendous vitality for you rallied at times until you seemed almost your old self, but always when the relapse came you sank a little deeper into the abyss that awaited you.

Then the shooting season opened. I am very positive that you were aware of it, for your knowledge of many, many things was always a source of wonder to me. Your eyes followed mv movements more closely during the hunting season, and once again I was keenly aware of them, even when you were apparently dozing before the fire.

Then one morning, after the frost had rimmed the lowlands with its white lace, you came to me with one of my hunting shoes in your mouth, and when I took it from you you went and found its mate. "Want to go, do you?" I asked, and with all the animation your spent body could summon you answered "Yes."

I am glad that I decided as I did. My life has been richer because of those few last hours we spent together in the woods. There was a cover by the river, a scant three miles from home, that always held a few woodcock. By jouncing the car for a mile over corduroy roads I could put you within a half mile of it, and I knew your gallant heart could carry you the rest of the way This day was yours. Nothing could take it from you.

You got down from the car like an old, old dog, but there was a crispness in the fall air, a heady odor to the moldering leaves which seemed to breathe new life into your emaciated frame. Your head came up, your questing nostrils searched the stirring air, and your lance-like tail assumed its old-time merriness.

You found a woodcock at the very edge of the cover, a second and third in a little depression near its center, and the fourth and last as we circled back to the outer edge. The legal limit was four, and we gathered them in with only four shells. Better than we had done on some other occasions you could recall, eh, old pal? But it was fitting that it should end thus, for they were the last woodcock your glorious nose would ever locate. When you came out with that last bird your hunting days were over. Finished. Done.

And you were done, too, old man. The fire which the day had kindled in you flickered and died as we started back, and your legs gave way beneath you. I gathered you up in my arms, an almost lifeless load, and started back toward the car.

We had almost reached it when all at once I felt you stiffen in my arms. For a moment a quick dread seized me, and then I knew. Your head was uplifted. Your heavy eyes had opened wide and assumed a new brightness. Your extended nostrils were expanded and drank the crisp air in quick, excited inhalations. Ruffed grouse! Somewhere in the thicket just ahead that mottled brown king of the uplands crouched, poised on taut sinews for its hurtling ascent. Ruffed grouse! Generations of your ancestors had lived and died in order that there might be inculcated in you an inher-ited instinct which made the scent of ruffed grouse the acme of all your physical senses. It was the excuse for your being. Without it you never could have lived.

I lowered you gently to your feet, a spent creature who had shot his bolt and who was well-nigh done to death by an hour's toil. You swayed in your weakness, but the magic of hot grouse scent was in your nostrils and it was still potent. The trembling left your legs, your head lifted and you took four cautious steps ahead. A pause, another infinitely cautious step and you had it, straight and true from the fountain head. You froze into immobility A pitiful caricature of the thing of fire and bronze you once were, but invincible still. You had nailed your grouse.

I pushed the gun forward and stepped up behind you, and in that moment we became omnipotent. We were gods who ruled that little kingdom of birch and alder and scented fir. You in your infallibility had located the quarry and I was possessed with the sure knowledge that no tumultuous ascent, no artifice of twisting or dodging which was his heritage could suffice it in this moment of its dire need. This thing had been foreordained. It was something which had to be.

The grouse came out on thundering wings, scattering the brown leaves beneath it with the wind from its takeoff. Upward it careened, a flashing, brown projectile, and your eyes watched the startled flight.

The nitro crashed, and the bird hung limply in the air for a moment, suspended by its own inertia, before it hurtled down to set up a spasmodic drumming with its spent wings.

"Dead bird," I said, and you went in and brought it out

to me, and I could see a bit of heaven shining in your eyes.

I like, too, to remember the few last minutes we were together. You lay on your bed covered by your blanket. The lethal dose of sleeping potion was already beginning to circulate in your veins. Your eyes were heavy, but in them there was a contentment and peace.

Then a little pointer pup, a liver-and-white replica of what you must have been before I saw you, came up ans sniffed a friendly greeting to you. Your eyes opened a trifle wider, and beneath your blanket your hard tail beat a friendly response. You extended your nose, sniffed your approval of the little stranger and bade him welcome. You knew there must always be other dogs, and so your great heart accepted him and shared with him with the one you loved. It was all that was left for you to give. Then you yawned slepily and closed your tired eyes.

So long, Pal.

SOURCES

Grateful acknowledgment is made to the authors and publishers for the use of the following material. Every effort has been made to contct original sources. If notified, the publisher will be pleased to rectify any omission in future editions.

Berendt, John. From *Midnight in the Garden of Good and Evil*, by John Berendt, copyright © 1994 by John Berendt. Used by permission of Random House, Inc.

Coughlin, Ruth Pollack. "Lucy Never Had a Bone to Pick" copyright © Ruth Pollack Coughlin. Originally published in *The Detroit News*, 1/13/1992. Reprinted with permission from *The Detroit News*.

Galsworthy, John. *Memories*. London, W. Heinemann; New York: C. Scribner's Sons, 1914.

Gasztold, Carmen Bernos de. "The Prayer of the Dog," from *Prayers From the Ark* by Carmen Bernos de Gasztold, translated by Rumer Godden, copyright © 1962, renewed © 1990 by Rumer Godden. Original copyright 1947, © 1955 by Editions du Cloitre. Used by permission of Viking Penguin, a division of Penguin Group (USA) Inc.

Hancock, Sunny. "Cowdogs, Generally Speaking" from *Cowboy Poetry of the Late Twentieth Century: Cattle, Horses, Sky, and Grass*, edited by Warren Miller. Flagstaff, AZ: Northland Publishing Co.

Herriot, James. "Do Dogs Have Souls" by James Herriot, copyright © 1983 by James Herriot. From *The Best of James Herriot* by James Herriot. Reprinted with permission of St. Martin's Press, LLC.

Hill, Gene. All Gene Hill stories copyright © Cathy Hill.

Macleod, Alistair. "Winter Dog" from *As Birds Bring Forth The Sun*. Copyright © Alistair Macleod. Toronto: McLelland Steward, 1986.

Paulsen, Gary. "Last Run" from *Puppies, Dogs and Blue Northers: Reflections on Being Raised by a Pack of Sled Dogs*. Copyright © 1996 by Gary Paulsen. Reprinted with permission of Harcourt, Inc.

Santee, Ross. "Wrinkle and I." Reprintd with the permission of Scribner, an imprint of Simon & Schuster Adult Publishing Group, from *Dog Days* by Ross Santee. Copyright © 1955 by Ross Santee; copyright renewed © 1983 by James W. Whitsell, Administrator of the Estate of Ross Santee.

Schaeffer, Susan. "The Dog." Copyright © Susan Schaeffer.

Spiller, Burton. "So Long, Pal" from *Drummer in the Woods*, [stories. 1st ed.]. Princeton, NJ: Van Nostrand, 1962.

Thurber, James. "The Dog That Bit People" from *My Life and Hard Times* by James Thurber. Copyright © 1933 Rosemary Thurber. "A Snapshot of Rex" from *The Middle-Aged Man on the Flying Trapeze* by James Thurber. Copyright © 1935 Rosemary Thurber. Reprinted by arrangement with Rosemary A. Thurber and The Barbara Hogenson Agency, Inc. All rights reserved.

Updike, John. "Dog's Death" from *Midpoint and Other Poems* by John Updike, copyright © 1969 and renewed 1997 by John Updike. Used by permission of Alfred A. Knopf, a division of Random House, Inc.

Vaughn, Stephanie. "Dog Heaven" from *Sweet Talk* by Stephanie Vaughn, copyright © 1990 by Stephanie Vaughn. Reprinted by permission of Georges Borchardt, Inc., for the author.

White, Randy Wayne. "The Legend" from *Batfishing in the Rainforest: Strange Tales of Travel & Fishing*, by Randy Wayne White. Reprinted by permission of Globe Pequot Press/Lyons Press.